ECONOMIC ISSUES, PROBLEMS AND PERSPECTIVES

THE EUROZONE: TESTING THE MONETARY UNION

ECONOMIC ISSUES, PROBLEMS AND PERSPECTIVES

Additional books in this series can be found on Nova's website under the Series tab.

Additional E-books in this series can be found on Nova's website under the E-book tab.

GLOBAL ECONOMIC STUDIES

Additional books in this series can be found on Nova's website under the Series tab.

Additional E-books in this series can be found on Nova's website under the E-book tab.

ECONOMIC ISSUES, PROBLEMS AND PERSPECTIVES

THE EUROZONE: TESTING THE MONETARY UNION

HANNAH J. FARKAS
AND
DANIEL C. MURPHY
EDITORS

Nova Science Publishers, Inc.

New York

337.142
FAR

For permission to use material from this book please contact us:
Telephone 631-231-7269; Fax 631-231-8175
Web Site: http://www.novapublishers.com

NOTICE TO THE READER

The Publisher has taken r easonable car e in the pr eparation of t his b ook, but makes no expr essed or implied warranty of any kind and assumes no responsibility for any errors or o missions. No liability is assumed for incidental or conse quential dam ages in connection with o r ar ising out of i nformation contained in this book. The Publisher shall not be li able for any special, consequential, or exemplary damages resulting, in whole or in part, from the r eaders' use o f, or r eliance upon, this material. Any parts of this book based on government reports are so indicated and copyright is claimed for those parts to the extent applicable to compilations of such works.

Independent verification sho uld be s ought for any data, advice or recommendations contai ned in t his book. In addition, no responsibility is assu med b y the publisher for any injury and/or da mage t o persons or property arising from any methods, products, instructions, ideas or otherwise contained in this publication.

This publication is designed to provide accurate and authoritative information with regard to the subject matter cover ed her ein. I t is sold with the clear under standing that the Publisher is not engaged in rendering legal or any other professional services. If legal or any other expert assistance is required, the services of a co mpetent per son sho uld be sought. FR OM A DE CLARATION OF PAR TICIPANTS JOINTLY ADOPTED BY A CO MMITTEE O F THE A MERICAN B AR ASS OCIATION A ND A COMMITTEE OF PUBLISHERS.

Additional color graphics may be available in the e-book version of this book.

LIBRARY OF CONGRESS CATALOGING-IN-PUBLICATION DATA

The eurozone : testing the monetary union / editors, Hannah J. Farkas and
Daniel C. Murphy.
    p. cm. -- (Economic issues, problems and perspectives)
  Includes bibliographical references and index.
  ISBN 978-1-61209-113-6 (softcover : alk. paper)
  1. Monetary unions--Europe. 2. Monetary policy--European Union countries.
3. European Union countries--Economic policy--21st century. 4.
International finance. 5. Financial crises. 6. United States--Foreign
economic relations--Europe. 7. Europe--Foreign economic relations--United
States. I. Farkas, Hannah J. II. Murphy, Daniel C.
  HG3894.E97 2011
  337.1'42--dc22
                                                                2010047065

Published by Nova Science Publishers, Inc. † New York

CONTENTS

PREFACE

Sixteen of t he Europ ean U nion's tw enty-seven m ember stat es sha re an economic and monetary un ion (E MU) w ith the eur o as a singl e c urrency. Based o n a gross dom estic pro duct (G DP) and global trad e a nd investment shares c omparable to the Unit ed S tates, t hese countries (col lectively referred to as the Eur ozone) are a m ajor player in the worl d econom y and can affec t U.S. econ omic an d po litical in terests in sig nificant ways. This n ew boo k provides b ackground i nformation and analysis on the fut ure of t he Euro zone and discusses its origins, rationale, economic significance, key pro visions and design challenges.

Chapter 1- Sixte en of th e Europ ean U nion's 27 m ember states sh are an economic and monetary un ion (E MU) w ith the eur o as a singl e c urrency. Based o n a gross dom estic pro duct (G DP) and global trad e a nd investment shares c omparable to the Unit ed S tates, t hese countries (col lectively referred to as the Eur ozone) are a m ajor player in the worl d econom y and can affec t U.S. econ omic and po litical inter ests in si gnificant w ays. G iven its e conomic and p olitical heft, t he ev olution a nd fut ure direc tion of the Euro zone is of major intere st to Co ngress, partic ularly com mittees wit h oversight responsibilities for U.S. international economic and foreign policies.

Chapter 2- O n May 2, 20 10, t he Eu rozone member states an d the International Monetary Fund (IMF) announced an unprecedented € 110 billion (about $145 bil lion) fina ncial assistance pac kage for Greece. The followi ng week, on May 9, 2010, E U leaders an nounced that they w ould make a n additional €500 billion (about $636 billion) in financial assistance available to vulnerable European countries, and suggested that the IMF could contribute up to a n a dditional €220 b illion to €250 billion (a bout $2 80 billion to $318 billion). This repor t a nswers freque ntly ask ed q uestions a bout IMF involvement in the Eurozone debt crisis.

Chapter 3- Over the past decade, Greece borrowed heavily in interna tional capital markets to fund governm ent budg et and current account defi cits. The profligacy of the government, weak revenue collection, and structural rigidities in Greece's ec onomy are typically cite d as m ajor factors behind Greece's accumulation of debt. Access to capital at low interest rates after adopting the euro and weak enforcement of EU rul es concerning debt and deficit ceilings may also have played a role.

In: The Eurozone: Testing the Monetary Union   ISBN: 978-1-61209-113-6
Editors: H.J. Farkas and D.C. Murphy   © 2011 Nova Science Publishers, Inc.

Chapter 1

THE FUTURE OF THE EUROZONE AND U.S. INTERESTS*

*Raymond J. Ahearn, James K. Jackson,
Rebecca M. Nelson and Martin A. Weiss*

SUMMARY

Sixteen of the European Union's 27 member states share an economic and monetary union (EMU) with the euro as a single currency. Based on a gross domestic product (GDP) and global trade and investment shares comparable to the United States, these countries (collectively referred to as the Eurozone) are a major player in the world economy and can affect U.S. economic and political interests in significant ways. Given its economic and political heft, the evolution and future direction of the Eurozone is of major interest to Congress, particularly committees with oversight responsibilities for U.S. international economic and foreign policies.

Uncertainty about the future of the Eurozone grew in early 2010 as a result of the onset of a sovereign debt crisis in Greece that was intensified by fears that the crisis could spread to other heavily-indebted Eurozone members.

---

* This is an edited, reformatted and augmented version of Congressional Research Service publication, Report R41411, dated September 14, 2010.

These concerns, i n t urn, t ook on a dded si gnificance be cause t he eur o is considered a cornerstone of the European integration process.

One important cause of t he crisis stem med from flaws in t he architecture of the currency union, including the fact that the EMU provides for a common central bank (the E uropean Ce ntral Ba nk or ECB), and thus a common monetary p olicy, bu t leaves fiscal p olicy up to t he m ember countri es. Wea k enforcement of fisca l discipline, o ver tim e, led t o risi ng p ublic de bts, contributing to the 2010 Eurozone debt crisis.

In respo nse, Europe an leaders a nd i nstitutions, b ackstopped b y the International Monetary Fund (IMF) and U.S. Federal Reserve Bank, adopted a large fi nancial stabili zation package in May 2010 t o calm markets and t o demonstrate European so lidarity. Current pro posals to reform the c urrency union center heavily on increasing fiscal poli cy coor dination in w ays that do not surrender members' fiscal po licy autonomy, or cede nat ional sovereignty to a Eur opean Uni on ins titution. These include bett er enforcement of fisca l discipline, po ssible creation of a perm anent fi nancial crisis m echanism, and active involvement of the ECB in sovereign debt management.

The ref orms, if im plemented, c ould s trengthen the f oundation of th e Eurozone and bolster confidence in the euro. Given that the currency union is largely a p olitical u ndertaking an d a major sym bol of Euro pean i ntegration, European leaders may be expected to support reforms which keep the currency union in tact. Moreover, the prop osals under c onsideration intro duce institutions an d p olicies t hat d id n ot exist pri or t o the crisis, a nd r epresent higher levels of integration and commitment to strengthening the EMU.

At the sam e time, a nu mber of factors could wea ken or even perhaps undermine t he susta inability of the Eu rozone. In th e ev ent of s overeign defaults by so me members, publ ic su pport in fisc ally sou nd E urozone countries for resource transfers to high ly-indebted co untries co uld dec line. Shared responsibility for defaults could also lead to divisions among Eurozone members, causing s ome members to recons ider t he costs a nd benefits of membership. In addi tion, the fisc al problems so me Euroz one m embers face stem from economic imbalances that may be very difficult to resolve without a shift in economic policies by its members, particularly Germany.

If the Eur ozone survives l argely i n its current form or strengthens, the impact o n U.S. interes ts is like ly to b e minimal. However, if th e Eurozone were to break-up in a way that undermines the functioning of Europe's single market or resurrects na tional di visions, the im pact on U.S. econom ic and political interests could be significant.

INTRODUCTION

What has become known as the Eurozone crisis began in early 2010 when financial markets were shaken by heightened concerns that the fiscal positions of a n   umber of Euroz   one c ountries, beg inning   with G   reece, w   ere unsustainable.[1] Fears that   a possi ble Greek default   could spr ead to other Eurozone countries, particularly Irela   nd, Italy , Port ugal an d Sp ain, w ere exacerbated by revelations of banking sector weaknesses and a delayed policy response from European leaders and institutions. A fter extended negotiations, European leaders agreed in May 2010 to provide funding for a joint euro area loan facility for Greece and a broader on e for other euro area countries should they require loans.[2] Both loan packages were backstopped by various forms of assistance from the U.S. Federal Reserv e Board (FRB) and the Interna tional Monetary Fund (IMF).[3] Faced with a 1 5% depreciation of the euro against the dollar in the first half of 2 010, European pol icymakers began to foc us on th e need to address flaws in the architecture of the Economic and Monetary Union (EMU) of the European Union (EU).[4]

Most observers of the Eurozone believe that reform of the c urrency union is needed in order to b olster the e uro and avoid another fiscal cris is triggered by pu blic debt an d government defi cits. H ow the m embers of the Eurozone address this overriding chal lenge t o bolster the viability and st ability of the currency union, i n turn, h as ad ded si gnificance. U nlike i n c ountries suc h a s Argentina or Mexico, w here currency cri ses did n ot br ing i nto qu estion t he existence or survi val of t he state, t he euro bears weight in term s of Europe's political as pirations for   an " ever cl oser un ion." A s view ed by G erman Chancellor A ngela Merkel, "the currency uni on is . ... a q uestion, no more or less, of the pr eservation of the Eur opean idea ... for if the e uro fails, Europe fails."[5]

A broa d ra nge of vi ews e xists o n t he future of   the Euro zone. So me academics and j ournalists maintain t hat fears about t he l ong-term viability of the Eurozone are exaggerated. The most optimistic, in fact, see the crisis as an opportunity to ad vance the i dea of an 'ever closer union' by p ursuing greater economic int egration a nd jo int c oordination of fisc al p olicy o n the European level. Other academics and journalists maintain that a potential break-up of the currency union, in part or in w hole, c annot be rul ed o ut. Wh ile suc h a development would not necessarily lead to the demise of the European Union, most observers agree that a break-up would be destabilizing.

The Obam a Administration, Feder al Re serve (Fed), and Congress have been act ively enga ged in   monitoring and w   orking tow ards an orderly resolution of the E urozone crisis. In itially, a major U.S. con cern w as th at a sovereign default by Greece could have risked another wave of credit freeze-ups, i nstability in the E uropean b anking sect or, an d spill over to glo bal financial markets. Between February and May 2010, U.S. officials consistently urged t heir Eu ropean counterparts to provide fin ancial a ssistance to Gre ece and other vul nerable Europea n e conomies. T he Fe d reactivated t emporary swap lines to provide the ECB with liquidity should it be needed.

Congressional concerns centered on t he role that the IMF was pl aying in resolving th e crisis. O ther concerns h ave focuse d o n how slow er g rowth i n Europe m ay affect the U.S. economy, as well as on how the e volution of the currency union could affect the U.S.-European political partnership. Given its economic and poli tical im portance t o the Unite d Stat es, the e volution a nd future direction of th e Eurozone is of m ajor interest to Congress, p articularly committees with oversight responsibilities for U.S. international economic and foreign policies.

This report provides background information and analysis on the future of the Eurozone in six parts:

- the **first** part discusses t he origins, ra tionale, ec onomic signific ance, key provisions, and design challenges of the Eurozone;
- the **second** section describes how persistent economic imbalances are underlying ca uses of the Euroz one cri sis and analyzes how t he imbalances ar e relate d t o i nadequate adjustment m echanisms within the EMU;
- the **third** section foc uses on pro posals to defus e t he E urozone crisi s and strengthen the framework of the currency union;
- the **fourth** section examines three possible scenarios for the fut ure of the Eurozone: (1) the Eurozone br eaks apart, (2) the E urozone survives, and (3) the Eurozone becomes more integrated;
- the **fifth** secti on assesses t he im plications of t he E urozone crisis for U.S. economic and political interests; and
- the **sixth** and final section offers concluding observations.

BACKGROUND ON THE ECONOMIC AND MONETARY UNION (EMU)

EMU official ly stands for Econom ic and Mo netary U nion, b ut i t als o commonly referred to as the Euro pean Mo netary U nion. EM U is the agreement am ong part icipating c ountries of the E uropean U nion t o adopt a single currency, the eur o, a nd a c ommon monetary p olicy set by a common central bank, the European Central Bank.

Origins, Rationale, and Economic Significance

The ori gins o f EMU are closely li nked with th e in ternational m onetary system established after World War II. [6] As part of the post-war reconstruct ion efforts, countries returned to a gold standard an d crea ted a fixe d, but adjustable, sy stem of intern ational e xchange rates based on a fixe d exchange rate between the U .S. d ollar an d t he pri ce of gold. T he g oal w as to pro vide international monetary stab ility, facil itate trade, an d prevent t he competitive devaluations, unst able exchange rates, a nd prot ectionist trade pol icies of the interwar years. Whil e E uropean l eaders had begun t he pro cess of economic integration immediately fol lowing Worl d War II, c onsideration of monetary union did not begin in earnest until the international monetary anchor provided by the dollar-gold sta ndard col lapsed in 1971 a nd a n ew w ave of c urrency instability em erged amidst div ergent national p olicy respons es to severa l 1970s economic shocks, including the oil crisis.

In 19 79, the ni ne m ember co untries of the E uropean Ec onomic Community (EEC) creat ed the European Monetary System (EMS). T he EMS introduced fixed but adjustable e xchange rates among participating countries' currencies i n order to keep flu ctuations of th eir exc hange ra tes w ithin acceptable bands. In 1988, the E uropean C ommission, then led by Jacques Delors, chaire d a com mittee which proposed a three-stage pl an t o reach f ull economic union. The pl an inc luded the establishment of a E uropean ce ntral bank and a single currency that would replace national currencies.

The EMU officially began on January 1, 1999, when eleven EU m embers pegged their currencies at a fixed exchange rate in pre paration for adoption of a com mon currency, t he euro. Parti cipating countries have a c ommon ce ntral bank, t he E uropean Ce ntral Ba nk (EC B), and by ext ension a com mon monetary policy. Fiscal policy, or d ecisions about spending and taxation were left to the individual member states, subject to the 1997 Stability and Growth Pact.

The prim ary ration ale fo r the EMU w as to provi de momentum for political un ion, a lo ng-standing goal of many Eu ropean p olicymakers. Germany and France, E urope's l argest economies, pl ayed t he l ead role i n establishing th e EMU, but t hey have not al ways ag reed on th e m anagement and dire ction of the single currency. Mo st observers believe th at Germany's initial s upport for m onetary uni on was motivated more by po litical than economic interests – former Chancellor Helmut Kohl saw the currency union as an im portant way to anchor Germany securely in a united Europe. Frenc h leaders, on the other hand, are thought to have viewed the currency union as a key step t o increas ing French i nfluence wi thin Europe. Each cou ntry subsequently had differe nt prior ities in gu iding t he de velopment of th e monetary u nion. G ermany has insisted that t he Euro zone be anchored in a culture of tight money, low inflation policy, and fiscal discipline. Accordingly, the ECB's overriding c ommitment to pric e s tability is t hought to refle ct German preferences. For i ts part, Franc e has pushed f or more flexi bility i n European monetary poli cy and for m ore poli tical c ontrol ov er the i nflation-fighting ECB.[7]

Although po litical go als were the driving force in the move towards monetary u nion, d iscussions of EMU also foc used heavily on i ts e conomic costs and benefits. Generally, European monetary union was expected to make Europe's economy m ore e fficient, thereby raisi ng the l iving sta ndards of Europe. For example, it would el iminate the transaction costs of changing one currency i nto ano ther, w hich w ould benefit b oth co nsumers and pr oducers. Additional e conomic be nefits i ncluded lo wering the c ost of trading goods by removing exchange rate risk and c urrency conversion fees and, by facilitating price comparisons of goods and services across national borders. Cost savings that arise fro m greater com petition a lso in duce dire ct in vestment fro m non-Eurozone co untries as fore ign firm s atte mpt to l ocate facil ities wit hin th e Eurozone area to a ccess a larger market. Proponents of t he EMU a lso wanted the euro to become one of the reser ve currencies of int ernational finance, alongside the dollar and the yen.[8]

The now 16 members of the Eurozone have consi derable econom ic heft. Comprising some 320 million people, the gross domestic product (GDP) of the entire Eurozone area was $13.6 trillion in 2008,[9] or about 22% of world GDP. By com parison, the GDP of the Unite d States in 2008 was sli ghtly larger at $14.1 trillion. Within the E urozone, ec onomic weight i s heavily co ncentrated in a few larg e cou ntries. More th an 7 7% of the E urozone's t otal GDP is accounted for by j ust four countries (G ermany, France, Ita ly, a nd Spain). In contrast, the Eurozone's fi ve sm allest c ountries (i n de creasing s ize: Slovakia, Slovenia, L uxembourg, Cy prus, and Malta) acc ounted for less than 2% of the Eurozone's overall GDP in the same year.

The Eurozone is also a major player in the world ec onomy. As a whole, it accounted for 29% of total world exports; 28% of worl d imports; and 23% of world ne t infl ows of foreig n direc t in vestment (FD I) in 20 08.[10] The United States a lso has a stron g b ilateral ec onomic rel ationship w ith t he E urozone.[11] With r espect to tra de, U.S. ex ports to Euro zone m embers tot aled $ 162.7 billion in 2009, re presenting 1 5% of total U.S. exports. Likewise, the value of U.S. im ports fro m the Eurozon e in 2009 was $21 6.5 billion, or 13% of total U.S. im ports.[12] In t erms of capi tal flow s, U .S. in vestors on ne t re patriated $128.2 billion dollars from the Eurozone in 2009.[13]

Key Provisions of the EMU

The bl ueprint for the EM U w as form alized in provisions of t he 1992 Maastricht Treaty, the founding document of the present-day European Union. The Treaty established the conditions, or "convergence criteria," that countries are required to meet before they join the EMU.[14] By requiring the me mbers to adhere to s imilar economic po licies, t he converge nce crit eria are meant t o promote a m ore b alanced ec onomic gr owth and development a mong t he various members of the Eurozo ne. This, in turn, w as thought to make it easie r for diverse economies to share a single currency.

As an in tegral part of t he EMU, a Eur opean Ce ntral Bank (ECB) was established to set monetary policy independent of any political influence. The ECB together with the central banks of all the members of the European Union form the Euro pean Sy stem of Central Banks, or ESCB , which is ch arged by statute wi th maintaining pric e sta bility as i ts p rimary objec tive. T he formulation o f price sta bility as a pr imary ESCB obje ctive, c ompared to the U.S. Federal Reserve's multiple mandates of price stab ility, full e mployment, and m oderate lon g-term i nterest rates, was a Germ an pre-con dition for sacrificing the Deutsche mark.[15]

There was no provision i n the Maastricht Tre aty to allow the ECB to act as a lender of last resort to Eurozone members in the case of a financial crisis. According to the EMU's desi gn, ea ch member must fina nce its deficits by itself. A " no-bail-out" clause ex plicitly stipulates that ne ither t he European Union nor any member state is liab le for or can assum e the de bts of any other member state. [16] However, EU financial assista nce i s allowed i n case of "severe diffic ulties caused by natur al disasters or e xceptional occurrences beyond the control of a member state."[17]

EU TREATIES

The Treaty on European Union (TEU or t he Maastricht Treaty) is th e founding document of the modern European Union. Together, the TEU and the 1 957 Tre aty est ablishing the E uropean Ec onomic C ommunity (also known as the Rome Treaty or the EEC Treaty, and rec ently re-named the Treaty on th e Functi oning of the Euro pean U nion, or TFEU) define the objectives and pri nciples of th e EU a nd se t o ut the EU's insti tutional architecture and organizational rul es. T he Lis bon Tr eaty, w hich entered into forc e i n December 2009, is the m ost rece nt trea ty a mending t hese documents.

Consolidated versio ns of th e TEU and th e TFEU are avai lable i n the Official J ournal of th e E uropean U nion, Marc h 3 0, 2010, a vailable at : http://eur-lex.europa.eu/LexUriServ/LexUriServ.do?uri= OJ:C:2010:083:FULL:EN:PDF

For the m utual assura nce a nd st ability of the currency, all m embers are constrained in their ability to adopt independent fiscal policies by the Protocol on E xcessive Deficit Proc edure (EDP) and th e Sta bility a nd Gro wth Pac t (SGP). The ED P is a procedure under which m ember states are obli ged t o avoid e xcessive defi cits in nati onal budgets. [18] The S GP, agreed t o in 1997, was inte nded to de epen multilateral surv eillance an d " speed up a nd clarify" implementation of the EDP.[19]

Soon after the SGP took effect in 1999, EU members began criticizing the rules-based approach of t he Pact for being t oo strin gent a nd they q uestioned whether the rules could be enforced. In 2003, the weak nesses of the Pact were exposed w hen the Eur opean Co uncil v oted aga inst app lying the punitive procedures under t he EDP to France and Ger many, w hich had experi enced rising levels of gov ernment deb t. Som e EU members argue d th at the Pact focused to o h eavily on th e rules-bas ed p ercentage gu idelines wit hout regar d for the circ umstances under which a gover nment's level of d ebt or its defic it spending m ay rise, for insta nce as a result of a tem porary i ncrease in government spending to counter an economic downturn.[20]

In 2005, t he EU members adopted a num ber of changes to t he Sta bility and Growth Pact. These changes made enforcement more flexible to take into account the economic conditions of the member states, and other factors. F or example, the modified Pact provides for each EU m ember to develop i ts own medium-term objectives t o brin g its deficit spe nding and its de bt l evel i nto compliance b ased on the u nique economic c onditions of eac h m ember. T he changes a lso allow EU members to avoi d the c orrective measures in cases where their annual fiscal deficit exceeds 3% of GDP, if th ey can demonstrate that the deficit is caused by "exceptional and temporary" circumstances.

Design Challenges

From the sta rt of the eur o area, var ious academ ics and poli cymakers argued th at a singl e curre ncy for many different e conomies w ould fac e numerous challe nges an d so me even argued t hat it w as bou nd to fai l. According to these crit ics, a bi g wea kness of the pr oject was the l ack of a common fiscal policy to support it. This, in turn reflected the fact that it was a currency w ith a ce ntral b ank b ut w ithout a g overnment th at has taxation and spending authority. The creation of the euro als o meant that m embers of the Eurozone lost their ability to use monetary and exchange rate policy tools as a way to respond to changes in economic conditions.[21]

The loss of m onetary and e xchange rate tools, combined with a lack of a common fiscal policy, creates vulnerabilities and tensions because members of the Eurozone are constrained in how they respond to economic shocks such as a recession. Countries are different and i n a recessi on are likely to e xperience different unemployment rates. In a curre ncy uni on, the central bank will set a common inter est rat e t hat may end u p t oo high f or t he high unemployment country, resul ting in lost employment and o utput, a nd to o low for the l ow unemployment co untry, result ing in excess spend ing a nd c onsumption, a nd exacerbating the business cycle in both countries.

Despite these costs, joining a currency union may be advantageous as long as t here are adjustm ent mechanisms that ens ure that the benefi ts of membership such as l ower transac tion costs and e xchange ra te certa inty exceed the costs. Thes e adjustment mechanisms, in the absence of a common federal b udget an d ro bust t ransfer mechanisms fro m c ountries experiencing booms to t he co untries experiencing re cessions, include la bor and c apital mobility an d wage an d p rice flex ibility. For exa mple, the unemployment disparities co uld be redu ced i f wo rkers fro m a co untry wi th high unemployment relocated to the one with low unemployment. Or, relative labor costs could fall in the high unemployment country to attract investment and create new jobs. In the abs ence of viable adjustment mechanisms, there are likely to be strains and tensions within a currency union.[22]

The f unctioning of t he d ollar i n t he U.S. eco nomy, desp ite m ajor differences among its fifty states, is facilitated by adjustment mechanisms that are either absent or deficient in the Eurozone. For example, U.S. unemployed workers move much more freely fro m Maine t o Minnesota than do European unemployed workers m ove fro m Spain to Sl ovenia because of diffe rences i n language and regulations. Prices of basi c consumer durables vary little among the U.S. stat es but ca n be substantial a mong the m embers of the Euroz one. And the federal government in Wash ington c ollects roughly two-thirds of a ll taxes and provides n et fi scal transfer s to states wi th tem porarily falling incomes. No such substantial fiscal transfers occur in the Eurozone.[23]

Just as critical to lacking a c ommon federal budget to transfer resources from countries ex periencing b ooms to c ountries ex periencing re cessions, the single curre ncy can weaken the market signals tha t w ould o therwise w arn a member that its fiscal deficits were becoming excessive. When a country with excessive deficits needs to raise ta xes and cut governm ent spending, as many Eurozone co untries need t o now , the result ing c ontraction in output and employment cannot be moderated by a devaluation that increases exports and decreases im ports. T hese shortc omings or desig n flaw s inhere nt in t he architecture of the curre ncy uni on played a role i n th e soverei gn de bt crisis that hi t G reece and se veral other E urozone members in early 20 10 and are discussed in the next section.

ECONOMIC IMBALANCES AND ADJUSTMENT MECHANISMS WITHIN THE EUROZONE

At the tim e of the eur o's launch i n 1999, a num ber of econom ists predicted that the monetary union would not survive because of sh ortcomings in its arc hitecture. This secti on de scribes (1) th e persiste nt economic imbalances t hat are at t he heart of th e current cri sis; and (2) how th e imbalances ar e relate d t o t he ins titutional cons traints of the m onetary union itself, particularly the lack of adequate adjustment mechanisms.

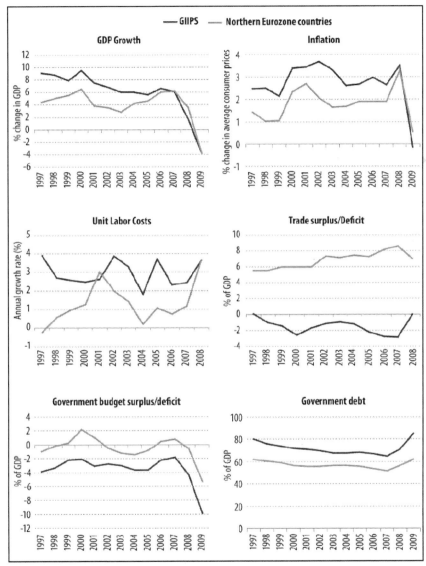

Source: G DP and inflation data are fro m the IMF' s World Econom ic Outloo k
database. Unit labor co st are fr om the So urce OECD database. Trade data i s from
the W orld Bank's W orld Development Indicators. Budget and debt data are from
European Co mmission, Direct orate Gene ral Economic and Financial Aff airs,
General Government Data, Part II: Tables by Series, Spring 2   010,
http://ec.europa.eu/economy_finance/db_indicators/gen_gov_data/documents/201
0/spring2010_series_en.pdf.

Notes: GIIPS refers to Gre ece, Ireland, Ital y, Portugal, and S pain. Northern Eurozone countries incl ude Austria, Bel gium, Germany, Finland, France, Luxe mbourg, and the Neth erlands. F our countrie s that h ave j oined the Euro z one in 200 7 or later (Cyprus, Malta, Slovenia, and   Slovakia) are n ot included. Un weighted a verages used. Unit labor costs (for the t otal economy) were used. Trade data are for goods and servic es. Budget data are   for general govern ment (cent ral, state, and local levels) as a percentage of GDP at market prices. Debt data are general government (central, state, and local l evels) consolidated gross debt as a percentage of GDP at market prices.

Figure 1. Economic Trends in the Eurozone.

Imbalances within the Eurozone

When the eu ro was in troduced, many eco nomists exp ected that   the national e conomies within th   e Eur ozone wou ld ach ieve add itional convergence. However, many of the Eurozone economies have remained quite different or h ave actually diverged in a number of eco nomic dimensions over the past decade. This divergence is generally thought to have occurred broadly between two grou ps of countries within the Eurozone: the Northern European countries, i ncluding A   ustria,   Belgium, Germ any, Finla nd, France, Luxembourg, and the N etherlands; and a group of m ostly Southern E uropean countries, including Greece , Ireland, I taly, Portuga l, a nd Spa in. Thes e la tter five countries are referred by the acronym "GIIPS" throughout this report.

Figure 1 shows average ec onomic trends in these two groups of c ountries over t he pas t deca de. Prio r to the o utbreak of th e gl obal fina ncial crisis in 2008, the GIIPS experienced higher rates of economic growth on average than the Northern European   countries. However, the   GIIPS also generally experienced faster grow th i n pric es (inflation), i ncluding faster grow th in the compensation for workers (adjusted for differences in wo rker p roductivity). This resu lted in a l oss of ind ustrial c ompetitiveness for the GIIPS and a   n increase in industrial competitiveness for the Northern European countries. As a result, the GIIPS on avera ge ran tr ade deficits, while the Northern E uropean countries general ly ran la rge trade surpl uses. T he GII PS also generally ran larger g overnment bud get defic its (rela tive to G DP) and ac cumulated hi gher levels of g overnment de bt (rel ative t o G DP) tha n N orthern European countries.

Much of t he money that the G IIPS bo rrowed to fi nance trade and budget deficits came fro m banks located in the Euro zone, p articularly Fr ench a nd

German banks.[24] The exposure of French and German banks to the GIIPS rose from $357.2 billion in December 1999 to $1.6 trillion in December 2009, an increase of more than 450%.[25] These sums, in turn, are in part a mirror image of the GIIPS and Northern European countries where the net borrowers are being financed by the net savers.

Adjustment Mechanisms

Differences between the economies of Northern Europe and the GIIPS can be attributed to a number of factors, including policy choices.[26] For example, Germany's export-led economic strategy and commitment to wage moderation is often cited as a factor for its low costs of production and trade surpluses.

However, many have suggested that the imbalances are caused by the institutional arrangements of the currency union itself and its inadequate adjustment mechanisms. This argument typically proceeds as follows:[27] After the GIIPS adopted the euro, investors viewed these countries as safer destinations for investment, and the interest rates paid by the GIIPS on their government bonds fell to the interest rates paid by Northern European countries. As a result, interest rates in the GIIPS were far too low, leading to distorted investment decisions and ultimately overinvestment in a number of sectors. As private sector borrowing and demand increased, the GIIPS launched investment projects to allow growth to take place with less inflation. This, in turn, required increased borrowing, particularly from banks in Northern European countries, and contributed to larger government budget deficits.

Capital inflows into the GIIPS fueled domestic demand, leading to high levels of growth, but also to inflation. Increasing prices in the GIIPS reduced their competitiveness, and consequently, caused the GIIPS to start running current account deficits (See **Figure 2**).[28] Each year's current account deficits added to the public and private aggregate debt of the GIIPS. As part of this process, the GIIPS accumulated foreign debt which rose close to 80% of GDP.[29]

Meanwhile, most Northern European economies did not face dramatic reductions in their interest rates upon joining the Eurozone and did not have substantial increases in capital inflows. Combined with fiscal policies that aimed to contain domestic demand, the Northern European countries as a result had lower inflation and remained more competitive than their GIIPS counterparts. Partly due to their relative competitiveness, the Northern

European c ountries were a ble to export to t he GIIPS and run large curren t account trade surpluses.[30]

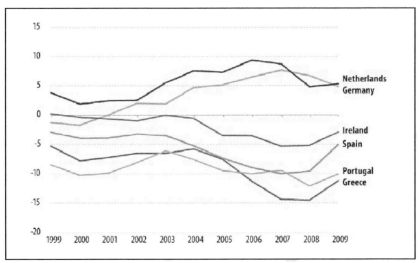

Source: International Monetary Fund

Figure 2. Selected European Current Account Balances Percent of GDP.

Some sugg est th at being i n th e E urozone c onstrained th e a bility of the GIIPS gov ernments to resp ond t o growing divergences fro m the Northern European countries.[31] For example, if the GIIPS had not been in the Eurozone, they could ha ve reduced th eir trade defi cits thro ugh currency depr eciation. Likewise, these observers argue, the GIIPS could have raised interest rates t o slow economic growth in response to a potentially over-heating economy. But for countries i n the E urozone, nei ther dev aluation n or a n incre ase in interest rates is an option.

The GIIPS did retai n some control over their fiscal policy and c ould have reined i n government sp ending or raise d ta xes i n order to curb co nsumption. Such a policy could have freed up resour ces for payments to foreign creditors. However, as discusse d p reviously, th e low interes t rates resulti ng fro m Eurozone membership inc reased t he at tractiveness o f governm ent defic it spending, and th e G IIPS cou ntries g enerally borr owed, ru nning b udget deficits. Alternatively, given that inflation was twice as high in the GIIPS than the EMU average, real interest rates (i .e., nominal rates minus inflation) were extremely low, thereby discouraging sa vings an d causing priv ate firms and households to run u p d ebt t o fin ance c onsumption an d ho using c onstruction, especially in Spain and Ireland.[32]

Given t heir membership i n t he Eurozone, the GIIPS are l eft wi th usi ng deflation (dec reases in wages, incom es, and prices) in order t o red uce their trade deficits. H owever, deflation m ay hav e l ittle beneficial effect on the foreign debt positions of most of the GIIPS if they all pursue the same strategy simultaneously. Th is i s because the negati ve effects on eco nomic g rowth and employment could be compounded, weakening the economies of the G IIPS to the point where their debt-to-GDP ratios continue to rise.[33]

In su m, the tr ade im balances betwe en t he N orthern countries an d G IIPS provide evide nce that t he EMU's int ernal a djustment mechanisms are not working wel l. Whatever la bor mobility a nd price fle xibility t hat e xists in t he Eurozone, combined with lim ited fisc al transfers, did n ot pre vent t he accumulation of persiste nt trade im balances a nd t he soverei gn debt crisis. While im proved labor m obility and price fl exibility may be lon g-term solutions, Eur opean lea ders and institutions are now considering a r ange of proposals t o i ncrease fisc al co ordination an d integration as the b est w ay t o shore-up the EMU's institutional shortcomings.

EUROZONE CRISIS MEASURES AND REFORM PROPOSALS

In May 2010, European leaders and institutions adopted an unprecedented package of e mergency measures to halt risin g fin ancial m arket t ensions stemming from concern a bout the fiscal solvency of G reece and se veral other Eurozone countries. This section first discusses the emergency crisis measures adopted by E U nat ional g overnments an d E uropean i nstitutions to d efuse the crisis. It then dis cusses r eform propos als for ec onomic go vernance and economic policies.

Table 1. Eurozone Emergency Crisis Measures

EU Loan to Greece	€80 billion
IMF Loan to Greece	€30 billion
European Financial Stability Facility (EFSF)	€440 billion
European Financial Stability Mechanism (EFSM)	€60 billion
Potential IMF contribution	€250 billion
ECB Purchases of Government Bonds	€61 billion (through September 8, 2010)

Sources: ECB, EU, IMF

Emergency Crisis Measures

Since the start of the Eurozone crisis, member governments have created a €110 bi llion f inance ass istance pr ogram for Greece, a €60 b illion E uropean Financial Sta bilization Mechanism (EFSM), and a €440 b illion European financial stability f acility (EFSF). Each facility is described below along with the roles pl ayed by the I MF and t he ECB in cr isis management. Thes e measures are summarized below in **Table 1**.

Greece Package

On May 2, 20 10, the Eur ozone m ember states a nd t he IMF anno unced a three-year, €110 bil lion fi nancial assistance package f or Greece (€80 b illion from member states and €30 b illion from the IMF). The Eurozone member states are providing assistance to Greece on a bilateral basis with the European Commission taske d ex clusively w ith coordinating an d managing the l oans. Eurozone m ember state l oans to Greece are structured bil aterally becaus e at the time of the a greement, ther e was no EU-leve l mechanism to provide balance of pa yments support to a Euroz one member co untry. In exc hange for the financial assistance, the Greek government has pledged to reduce Greece's government budget deficit from 13.6% of GDP in 2009 to below 3% by 2014. The IMF has referred to this program as un precedented i n t erms of the adjustment effort required by the government.[34]

Despite the announcement of the Greek package on May 2, 2010, financial market pressures continued to worsen over the ensuing days as the value of the euro de clined, stock m arkets decli ned, an d bo nd sprea ds of several southern European co untries wi dened sh arply ov er t he fo llowing week s. On May 1 0, 2010, EU officials announced a rescue package of up to €750 billion to restore confidence in EMU members' fiscal sus tainability. This co nsists of two ne w European fi nancing e ntities, t he E uropean Fin ancial Stab ility M echanism (EFSM) and the European Financial Stability Facility (EFSF). The IMF is also expected t o m ake c ontributions as well as play a co ordinating r ole, as it has much e xpertise i n fi nancial surve illance and p utting together so vereign debt packages.

European Financial Stability Mechanism

The EFSM is a new €60 b illion supra national EU bal ance of pay ments loan facility available to any EU member country facing financial difficulties. It is si milar i n desi gn t o an exis ting €50 bil lion EU bal ance of pa yments facility th at c an o nly be drawn on by n on-Eurozone EU member nations.[35] Since 2008, Hungary, Latvia, and Romania have borrowed from this facility as part of joint EU-IMF economic adjustment programs.

Under the new EFSM, the European Commission is allowed to raise up to an additional €60 billion on the international capital market by issuing bonds individually a nd collectively bac ked by all 27 EU m ember stat es.[36] EFS M loans req uire a qua lified majority vot e of the C ouncil of th e EU. The borrowing nation would be subj ect to eco nomic conditionality supervised by the E uropean Commission, w hich w ould decide at re gular i ntervals w hether sufficient ec onomic progres s has been m ade to w arrant the continued rel ease of funds. Funds are available im mediately and there is no sunset date for t he EFSM. To date, no country has requested funds from the EFSM.

European Financial Stability Facility

European lea ders dec ided t o pro vide th e majority of the rescu e pa ckage, up to €440 million, in a temporary three-year crisis prevention facility, the so-called European Financial Stability Facility (EFSF), outside of the EU system. The EFSF has been es tablished under L uxembourg law as a lim ited liability corporation.[37] This a llows participating countries to have gre ater discretion over th e use of the faci lity's resources – decisi ons are made by a board of directors from parti cipating countries ins tead of the Eu ropean C ommission – and to limit their l iability t o th e am ount of the ir in dividual g uarantee. T he amount of a co untry's g uarantee is   to b e d erived fro m their   respective contributions to the paid-in capital of the ECB.

If a country needs to borrow from the facility, it can leave the EFSF for a period of tim e per unanimous a greement of t he rem aining participants. T his agreement has already been reached for Greece. Eurozone member states have committed to prov ide a 1 20% guarantee of th eir sh are to e nsure sufficient capital in cas e other co untries nee d it. It is expected t hat th is facil ity will be used only under strict conditions of conditionality in order to minimize the risk of moral hazard.[38]

As it is currently structured, the EFSF   is a te mporary fac ility that will expire i n 2 013. W hether this crisis m echanism, which m ay operate   as a Eurozone version of the IMF, should be made permanent is the subject of on-going dis cussions. Th e pr ocedures or criteria t hat w ill be use d t o identify circumstances un der w hich co untries w ill be a llowed to   borrow f rom the facility is also a work in progress.

Participation of the International Monetary Fund

The IMF is expe cted to pa rticipate in any loans made by the EFSM and EFSF, and to provide at least half as m uch as the EU contribution, potentially up to €250 billion (half of the combined €60 billion EFSM and €440 billion EFSF).[39] The IMF, how ever, can not pre-com mit fun ds for a group of countries. Any IMF contributions to loan packages for Eurozone members will be on a co untry-by-country basis. A ny such loan would also be subject to the approval of t he IMF Exec utive Board in the same manner as al l IMF lending arrangements. In the case of the EFSF, the IMF is to play a role in determining whether a c ountry's fiscal si tuation merits assistance. If it d oes, the IMF must also approve a consolidation plan.

European Central Bank Response

Along with the creation of the EFSM and the EFSF, the European Central Bank has im plemented several crisis-response m easures to im prove European financial sta bility. Arguab ly the most important of t hese m easures is the ECB's decision to purchase European sovereign debt outright in the secondary markets. This w as a signifi cant pol icy reversal for the ECB, w hich had l ong viewed in terventions i n sovere ign de bt markets as com promising i ts independence, and a d iversion from its core mandate of pric e stab ility. However, as it required several months to legally establish the EFSM and the EFSF, the ECB was able to provid e i mmediate support following the worsening of the crisis in early May. The ECB began interventions on May 10, 2010, purchasing €16.5 billion of Euro zone sovereign debt.[40] As of July 20, 2010, the ECB held around €60 billion of European government bonds.[41]

The ECB als o create d a col lateral wai ver for Greece so tha t Greek sovereign de bt can be use d as coll ateral for loans to t he Europe an banking system. Under previo us ru les, G reek b onds w ould no l onger ha ve be en accepted by the ECB, putt ing addit ional pressure on the Europe an ba nking system.

Other ECB policy measures include the reactivation of temporary liquidity swap lines with the U.S. Federal R eserve. In addi tion to the ECB, t he Fed re-activated t emporary rec iprocal c urrency agre ements, known as swap lines, with the Bank of Cana da, the Bank of En gland, Bank of Japan, a nd the Swiss National B ank.[42] Th e swap li nes wi th the Fe deral Reserve pr ovide foreign central banks with a sour ce of dolla r finan cing s hould s uch immediate liquidity be n eeded. Si nce t heir rea ctivation, the use of thes e sw ap lines h as been very limited.

Economic Governance Reforms

Crisis response measures have succeeded in stabilizing financial markets, but they are temporary measures that do not address fundamental weaknesses in th e arch itecture of the EMU. Th e te mporary measures, how ever, hav e provided European leaders with time to consider changes in the governance of the curre ncy un ion. In itial pro posals have centered on de veloping m ore effective m eans of coordinati ng national fiscal policies and on pr omoting faster an d m ore bal anced g rowth. T hese preliminary proposals are d escribed briefly below.

Fiscal Policy Reforms

As discussed earlier, there is pressure to reform the current framework for European fis cal policy coordination. O n Ju ne 17, 2010, th e C ouncil of European Heads of State released a synopsis of current proposals for reform of the Stability and Growth Pact.[43] On surv eillance, leaders agreed to give public debt an d de bt susta inability issues a m ore pro minent ro le i n bu dgetary surveillance. EU leaders a greed t o a national bu dgets peer revi ew sy stem under whic h governments will su bmit t o th e Euro pean C ommission draf t budgets for peer review and coordination before they are finalized. EU leaders also agreed to sanctions, in principle, for countries with excessive debt levels, but d id not specify w hat form these sanctions w ould ta ke. France and Germany have pro posed s uspending th e vo ting ri ghts of Euro pean U nion members wh o persist ently exce ed b udget deficit l imits, but n either t he suspension of voti ng rights, nor aut omatic sancti ons w ere agree d at the Ju ne 2010 European C ouncil su mmit. The IM F has also argued t hat the E uropean Union n eeds to stre ngthen the enf orcement proc edure, in cluding sanctions, when countries are violating deficit limits.

Additionally, a tas k force on economic go vernance h eaded by H erman Van Rom puy, President of the Euro pean Council, will issue its fi nal report in October 2010, presenting recommendations for im proving the management of European ec onomic pol icies. EU lea ders are e xpected t o consider ot her proposals at a sum mit on O ctober 27- 29, 2 010. C ontroversial issues bei ng discussed, in additional t o possi ble sa nctions a nd t he suspension of voti ng rights, incl ude: (1) crea ting a Europe an regul atory mechanism to facil itate sovereign de bt restruct urings;[44] (2) issui ng Euro bonds;[45] a nd (3) creati ng a permanent European crisis fund when the EFSF expires in three years.

All three of t hese m easures address a key issue, the Maastri cht Treaty's "no ba ilout clause," w hich proh ibits t he EU or member sta tes fro m bein g liable for the obligations of other member states. However, with the creation of the EFSF, a precedent has been establis hed that Eurozone countries may be willing to pool resources and provide a centralized emergency fiscal backstop to a member country in excha nge for enhanced surveil lance a nd macroeconomic conditi onality. While the EFSF is te mporary, and limited to Eurozone countries, it could lead to permanent measures intended to create a more fiscally secure Europe.

Economic Growth Policies

Important for securin g th e lon g-term viabi lity of th e EMU is reversing several y ears of w eak e conomic grow th. The Ec onomic Inte lligence U nit forecasts a E urozone e conomic growth rate at 0. 7% for 2010 and 0.8% for 2011, while the IMF analy sis forecasts GDP growth at around 1% in 2010, increasing only to 1.2 5% in 201 1.[46] Because higher rates of eco nomic growth may help a void fut ure d ebt cr ises, priority is being g iven to addressing structural problem s such a s labor a nd service sector barriers, as well as t o macroeconomic poli cies and surve illance for pro moting stronger and more balanced economic growth.

For all Euro zone countries, the ECB a nd the Euro pean Commission have stressed th e i mportance in their v iew of pressin g forw ard w ith difficult structural ref orms that ha ve prevented the com pletion of t he European common market. Removing remaining trade barriers, especially in the services sector, is viewed by the ECB and the EC as being particularly important for increasing growth. A ccording t o t he E CB, on ly 20 % of servic es pr ovided i n the EU have a cross-border dimension. A full implementation of the European Commission's services li beralization prop osals co uld incre ase E U GD P growth rates by 0.6-1.5 percentage points.[47] Other growth enhancing EU-wide reform efforts incl ude pr omoting a com mon energy market and acc elerating the im plementation of n ew dig ital t echnologies i n acc ordance with the objectives of the Europe 2020 growth strategy.

Proposals o n strict er macroeconomic surveil lance s pecify the use of a scorecard for assessing c hanges i n competitive posit ions and flagging emerging m acroeconomic im balances in a tim ely fashion. While t hese proposals sti ll ne ed to be fl eshed o ut, it i s un clear how th ey w ill ad dress the current account imbalances within the Eurozone. In this context, much concern and weight may be pl aced on Germany, the largest economy of the E urozone, to increase internal dem and an d thereby buy m ore goo ds a nd s ervices of t he GIIPS as they become more competitive.[48] Recent movements in the exchange value of the euro are boosting e xports fro m Euroz one c ountries, b ut th e benefits are not being shar ed e qually a mong t he E urozone m embers. Since movements in the e xchange val ue of t he euro do not a ffect the com parative levels of pro ductivity am ong Eurozone members, those members w ith hi gher levels of productivity, such as Germany, tend to benefit the most. To the extent that ot her E urozone m embers are sim ilarly look ing t o spur t heir eco nomic growth by increasing exports, they likely will provide little stimulus to Greece and Spain or to other Eurozone members.

From a different perspective, many Germ ans reject t he not ion that the ir exporting success and trade surpluses come at the expe nse of fellow Eurozone members. They argue that e xports all ow the German economy to grow faster, and in the p rocess a bsorb more im ports fro m their Euroz one n eighbors. Furthermore, they maintain that other Eurozone countries, such as Gre ece and Spain, can increase their competitiveness just as Germ any has done by cutting costs and making specialized products.[49]

POSSIBLE SCENARIOS FOR THE FUTURE OF THE EUROZONE

The current debt crisis has arguably posed the most fundamental challenge to t he E urozone si nce the euro w as in troduced a decade a go a nd has led to speculation a bout t he fu ture of th e Eu rozone. T hree s cenarios have typica lly been d iscussed: (1) the cr isis l eads to a sp lintering or break-up of the Eurozone, with on e or more members abandoning the euro; (2) t he Eurozone survives t he crisis larg ely i ntact, wi thout m ajor reforms; and (3) s ubstantial reforms to the Eurozone a   rchitecture are im plemented, l eading t o great er economic and poli tical i ntegration. The outcome of t he crisis wil l like ly be influenced by a host of factors, incl uding market confidence, com mitments to reform packages, and the willingness of Eurozone member states to relinquish greater control over economic issues to the European level, among others.

Scenario 1. The Eurozone Breaks Apart

It w as onc e cons idered unthinkable t hat countries w ould le ave th e Eurozone, but the debt cris is facing se veral southern Euro pean count ries has raised th e possibility that one or m ore cou ntries c ould exit the E urozone. Exiting t he E urozone wou ld en tail c ountries a bandoning th e e uro as th eir national curre ncy, issuing a new nat ional currency, and al lowing the new national currency to appreciate or depreciate against the euro.

Exit by One or More Southern European Countries

Typically, th e discussi on a bout th e Euro zone brea king apart foc uses on one or m ore southern Eur opean c ountries deci ding t o lea ve th e Euroz one. There has also been som e discussion about southern European countries being pushed out of the Eurozone by northern European countries. For example, as European leaders discussed the response to the Greek de bt crisis, it is reported that i n March 20 10, G erman Chancellor A ngela Mer kel ta citly e ndorsed a proposal that would allow weak Eurozone member states to be "ejected" from the Eurozone.[50]

Perhaps the st rongest m otivation for so uthern E uropean co untries t o exi t the Eurozone w ould be to all ow t heir r esulting new national curre ncies t o depreciate against the e uro. This would help the southern European countries regain competitiveness against the northern European countries, likely leading to an increase in their exports and a decrease in their imports. It is argued that a surge in e xports w ould s pur e conomic grow th an d offset t he effe cts of the austerity m easures b eing undertaken by southern Eur opean c ountries to pay down their d ebt. It is a lso t hought t hat t hese new national currencies w ould help to correct the trade imbalances that have developed within the Eurozone and, as sou thern Eu ropean countries borrowed to finance th eir t rade deficits, that have co ntributed to th e accu mulation o f debt in these co untries over the past decade.

Exiting t he Eurozone wo uld in volve potentially h uge costs fo r the southern E uropean ec onomies, how ever, for at leas t fo ur reasons. Fi rst, the debt of sout hern European countries is d enominated in euros, a nd leaving the Eurozone in favor of a depreciated n ational c urrency c ould significantly raise the v alue of th eir debt in t erms of national currency. Second, t here are technical and legal obstacles to e xiting the euro.[51] Legislation would likely be required to issue the new na tional currency, and al l contracts i nvolving euros would h ave t o b e rew ritten for the national cu rrency. Nu merous el ectronic machines i nvolving e uros, incl uding co mputers, A TMs, an d ve nding machines, w ould have to be repr ogrammed or repla ced, an d n ew prin ting presses w ould be nee ded. Third, as i nvestors and co nsumers antic ipated th at the new national currency would depreciate in value against the euro, massive capital fli ght from the cou ntry cou ld trigger a m ajor finan cial cris is in t he country and put p ressure on o ther v ulnerable Eu ropean countries. This co uld have ne gative im pacts o n eco nomic grow th, at le ast in t he s hort ru n.

According t o one bank's estim   ates, for exam ple, a Greek exi   t fro m the
Eurozone would push output 7.5 percentage points lower in 2011 than initially
forecasted f or Greece, and 1 perce ntage point l ower for the other Eurozone
countries.[52] Fourth, leaving the Eurozone would likely also strain the country's
political rela tions w ith o ther cou ntries i n th e Euro pean U nion, and co uld
possibly even lead to the country having to depart from the EU.

Exit by One or More Northern European Countries

Another variant of the Eurozone-breaking-apart scenario is e xit by one or
more norther n Euro pean c ountries due to frustra tion with t he current debt
crisis.[53] Whe n th e E urozone w as crea ted, there w as c oncern among n orthern
Eurozone members, particu larly Germany, about the c ommitment of the EC B
to price st ability a nd the c ommitment of the so uthern European c ountries t o
sustainable debt levels. N orthern Euro pean c ountries did not w ant to be a
"fiscal b ackstop" for the s outhern Eur opean c ountries.[54] T o a ddress thes e
concerns, t he ECB was   c reated wit h the primary goal of price stability
(compared, f or exam ple, to t he U .S. Federal Reserve, w hich has a du al
mandate of price sta bility and full employment), the le gal text establishing the
euro included a " no b ail-out" cl ause, a nd limits were p ut in p lace o n t he
governments' overall outstanding debt levels (60% of GDP) and annual budget
deficits (3% of GDP).

However, t he current   debt crisis has   thrown t hese commitments int o
question. S ome ha ve argued that t he ECB's decis ion to buy E urozone p ublic
debt represe nts a loss of i   ndependence for the ce   ntral ban k, a nd political
support in some of the northern Eurozone countries for the financial assistance
package for the vulnerable Eurozone c ountries has, at times, bee n ambivalent
at b est. Som e hav e su ggested t hat o ne or more northe rn Euro pean countries
could exit the Eurozone in favor of a new n ational currency. In Germany, four
academics are act ively trying to chal lenge the consti tutionality of Germany's
membership in the Eurozone in German courts.[55]

Even if reve rting t o a new nat ional c urrency c ould re gain northern
European countries greater control over their monetary policy and reduce their
financial commitments to t he s outhern Euro pean co untries, leaving t he
Eurozone co uld b e cost ly. A new nati onal curre ncy for one of the north ern
European countries would l ikely ap preciate against the euro, com plicating the
export-led growth strat egies that se veral northern E uropean c ountries pursu e.
The no rthern Eu rozone coun tries wou ld also fac e the same technica l, le gal,
and po litical cha llenges to exi ting the euro that fac e t he southern E urozone
countries, discussed a bove. H owever, so me observ ers be lieve that banks in

northern E uropean c ountries, eve n w ith new na tional currencies, could s till accept debt paym ents in e uros fro m s outhern Eur opean c ountries without posing a risk to the ir solv ency.[56] This s cenario woul d also have signific ant repercussions for the EU and the future of European integration.

Scenario 2. The Eurozone Survives

A secon d p ossible s cenario is tha t the E urozone emerges from the crisis largely in its current form. The status quo in the Eurozone could be maintained if market pres sures on vul nerable southern European c ountries are c almed by the m agnitude of t he fi nancial assistance package, the ECB's pl edge to buy Eurozone p ublic debt, an d the in troduction o f new au sterity p ackages i n th e southern Eu rozone co untries. Th e au sterity and struct ural reform s could als o successfully lower prices in southern European countries, reducing imbalances within the Eurozone and obviating the need for additional integration of fisc al policies at th e Euroz one l evel. So me argue th at t he Eurozo ne co uld e ven survive a Greek de bt restructuring, which some market partic ipants believe is inevitable.[57] They argue t hat the f inancial ass istance fro m the IMF and t he other Eurozone member states will allow the restructuring to be delayed for a few years, when markets may be calmer and growth has been restored in other Eurozone member states. T his c ould a llow the restruct uring to be carried out in a n orderly fashion t hat would n ot ris k spe culation against ot her Eurozone countries and could allow Greece to remain in the Eurozone.

Some have e xpressed c oncern that if t he Eurozone do es em erge from the crisis i n its current form, the un derlying problems with the architecture of th e Eurozone t hat le d t o the c urrent cr isis w ould not be addressed. I n t his view, failure to address these issues, including coordination of fiscal policies at the European le vel a nd c orrection of t he imbalances withi n t he E urozone t hat developed over the past 1 0 y ears, m ay mean that similar crises lie ahead. On the o ther han d, sever al fin ancially vul nerable Eu ropean co untries, in cluding Greece, Irela nd, a nd Spai n, ha ve rec ently he ld suc cessful bond offerings, suggesting that the crisis m ay be sta bilizing. This m ight also be viewed as a n indication that this se cond scenario, the Eurozone survives in its current form, may be a likely outcome.

The new i nstitutional arran gements bei ng pro posed clearly fall s hort of a fiscal or political union that many economists be lieve is necessary to k eep the currency union together, whether they wil l be sufficient to st rengthen the euro area remains uncertain. Much could depend on whether financial markets have confidence i n the soundness of t he reforms implemented or whether markets are left won dering if reform s will lea d to m ore sustaina ble fis cal positions. Perceptions o n whet her t he Euroz one wi ll b e ab le to handle th e n ext cris is more efficient ly could de termine the l ong-term surviva l of t he E MU. Lit tle support exists in Europe for proposals that would imply a si gnificant transfer of spe nding a nd taxing powers to a ce ntral EU government a nd pa rliament. Today, the EU budget represents about 1% of EU GDP and proposals to boost that by even 0.1% consistently draw vetoes from several EU members.

Scenario 3. The Eurozone Becomes More Integrated

A third p ossible s cenario is th at s ubstantial ref orms to the Eur ozone architecture are i mplemented, leading to grea ter e conomic and political integration. This scenario would entail implementing reforms to reduce fisc al free-riding a nd t o e nhance the ability of the Euro zone to resp ond to fu ture crises, if and when they arise. Greater fiscal federalism and a clear mechanism to provide emergency financial assistance to v ulnerable countries would also be a goal. Several proposals, as discussed in the previous section, are currently being de veloped and are under c onsideration that are intended to accomplish these goals, including review of nat ional budgets at the European level, more stringent e nforcement of the restric tions on debt and d eficit l evels u nder the Stability and Growth Pac t (suc h as automatic e nforcement of financial sanctions or revo king vo ting rights of m ember states in vi olation of the Stability an d Growth Pact), and es tablishing a perm anent fun d to provide financial assistance to Eurozone m embers experie ncing bala nce of payment problems.

To date, proposals are still in the early stages. Control over fiscal policies remains at t he national level and fi nancial assistance to Eurozone members is being made available on a temporary (three year) bas is. Fiscal policies are a n important issue of nat ional sovere ignty, and it remains to b e seen w hether, or to what e xtent, n ational g overnments i n the E urozone will b e will ing to concede control over national budgets to European authorities. Also, given the unpopularity of the financ ial assista nce pac kage for Greece and t he broa der support mechanisms for vulnerable Eurozone members with voters in northern European countries, it is unclear whether countries will be will ing to commit, on a p ermanent basis, to providing financial assistance to Euro zone members in crisis.

Some observers argue for the crea tion of a so lid fra mework for crisis resolution and an ability to deal with sovereign default by a m ember state. In this view, the principle that a member state cannot fail may imply a political or fiscal union to underpin the euro.[58] These observers might also argue t hat the EU sh ould be abl e to i ssue so vereign debt. It i s un clear, ho wever, whether there is political will to do that.[59]

IMPLICATIONS FOR U.S. INTERESTS

Europe's response to the Eurozone cris is may affect U.S. econom ic a nd political interests in im portant w ays. The O bama A dministration, the Federal Reserve, and Congress have been engaged in monitoring and working towards an orderly res olution of the crisis. Ini tially, a m ajor U.S. co ncern w as that a sovereign default by G reece could have risked another wave of credit freeze-ups, instability in t he Euro pean banking sect or, a nd spill-over t o U.S. an d global financial markets. Currently, concern is centered on how slower growth and a weaker euro may affect the U.S. economy, as well as how the evolution of the currency union may affect U.S.-EU economic and political ties.

Economic Implications

Given the ti ghtening of fiscal policies thro ughout the E urozone i n response to t he crisis, som e econom ists are predic ting a continuing decline in the value of the euro vis-à-vis the dollar and slower growth over the next few years.[60] Over time, a stronger dol lar relative to the euro would likely translate into an increase i n the U. S. trad e deficit wi th the E urozone as European exports bec ome cheaper a nd U.S. e xports be come more expens ive. A larger U.S. t rade defi cit wi th th e Eu rozone, combined wi th e xpected in creased in U.S. trade def icits with Ch ina a nd ot her Asian c ountries, c ould increase t he U.S. current account deficit beyond its previous record of $800 billion in 2006.

To maintain its econom ic recovery und er these circumstances, the Uni ted States again may have to become the c onsumer and borrower of last resort (by running large bud get d eficits w ith d ebt-financed co nsumption susta ined o r facilitated by huge i nflows of forei gn purc hases of Treas ury bills , there by facilitating l ow interes t rat es). Under t his scen ario, t he stra tegy f or gl obal rebalancing of production and consumption agreed to by the Group of 20 at its last few meetings m ight n ot be re alized and pr otectionist pressure s in th e United States, with un employment rem aining high, co uld rise.[61] Lo w interest rates could, at the same time, facilitate Treasury Department efforts to finance high U.S. debt levels.

A weaker eur o woul d als o like ly have some effects on U.S.-Eurozone foreign direct investm ent flows. Curre ntly, Euroz one countries acc ount for 26% of a ll U .S. dire ct investment a broad a nd for 44% of a ll fore ign direct investment in the U nited States . Base d on sl ower pro jected growth rates in Europe, U .S. inv estors m ay look towards em erging m arkets for addi tional investments, parti cularly since pr ofits generated i n eur os w ould tran slate i nto fewer dollars, hurting the bottom line of U.S. paren t companies. An offsetti ng factor could be that European stocks and assets with a weaker euro would look cheaper and more attrac tive, parti cularly gi ven t hat t he average E uropean stock curre ntly sells for te n tim es estim ated 20 10 earnings -- t he l owest valuations b ased on expected ear nings si nce the 1980s and at a l evel tha t is 25% less than the average of U.S. stocks.[62]

The ec onomic im pact co uld be m uch more subst antial if the E urozone were to break-up or spl inter due to a deepening so vereign d ebt crisis. By one estimate, a complete break-up of the Eurozone could lead to a 10% cumulative loss o f ou tput ov er th e fi rst t wo years. [63] C ombined with a l ikely ad verse impact o n the funct ioning o f the EU 's singl e market, U.S. exports of go ods, services, an d investment to Europ e (w hich t otaled o ver $1.5 billion in 2 008) could be si gnificantly red uced. M oreover, suc h a d evelopment co uld also weaken he avily-exposed E uropean banks, parti cularly French a nd German banks, and precipitate another global financial crisis.[64]

At the sam e time, it is a lso p ossible that c urrent dif ficulties th e U.S. economy is facin g – sl ower than expected economic grow th and high unemployment – co uld c ombine w ith a bett er th an ex pected grow th performance in Europe to dilute the pressures for a weaker euro. The Eurozone economy, for exam ple, gre w faster tha n the U.S. e conomy (1% com pared to 0.4%) i n the seco nd q uarter of this year. [65] G iven t hat m any different factor s affect rel ative exc hange ra tes, predictions of l ong-term changes are ofte n inaccurate.

Political Implications

Over t he y ears, a key U .S. po litical interest has been a prosperous, peaceful a nd stabl e Europe. In suppor t of this i nterest, suc cessive U.S.

administrations have su pported Euro pean efforts at econ omic and poli tical integration. U.S. policy on the euro and the EMU has generally been that if it is goo d for Europ e, it w ill be goo d for the U nited St ates. For exa mple, o n January 4, 1999, then President Clinton issued the following statement:[66]

> We welcome the launch of the Euro, an historic step that 11 nations have taken toward a more complete Economic and Monetary Union (EMU). The United States has long advocated for European integration, and we admire the steady progress that Europe has de monstrated in taking the often difficult budget decisions that make this union possible. A strong and stable Europe, with open markets and robust growth, is go od for A merica and good for the world. A suc cessful economic union that c ontributes to a dynamic Europe is clearly in our long-term interests.

Given this h istory, if t he Eurozone em erges from the crisis close to its present form or even str onger tha n befo re, strong U. S.-EU politi cal ties are likely to co ntinue. Only in the possi ble scenari o of the Euroz one breaki ng apart are the effects li kely to ra ise questions about th e st atus q uo. Ma jor challenges to political ties c ould em erge if a break-u p of the Eur ozone w ere accompanied by growing divisions between key European countries, economic and s ocial turmoil in sel ected co untries, or a ret urn to m ore nat ionalistic policies. Th e O bama A dministration, l ike previ ous a dministrations, beli eves that a prosperous, secure, and increasingly integrated Europe that is capable of partnering with the Uni ted States in addressing mutual pol icy challenges is in the U.S. in terest. On the other hand, it might also be argued that if a break-up were to occ ur, the U nited St ates m ight have greater influence w ith in dividual members of the EU . Those who held t his view might also argue that a break-up could make the EU less of a rival to the United States.

CONCLUDING OBSERVATIONS

The E urozone crisis has highlighted c racks i n t he architecture of the currency union. Efforts to make th e cu rrency un ion more st able and sustainable i n the lo ng run represent on e of the m ost fundam ental c hallenges European leaders have faced in an over 50-year effort to advance political and economic integration. The U.S. stake in the outcome of these efforts, given the magnitude of U.S. economic and political ties with Europe, is considerable.

European proposals to date to reform the currency union center heavily on increasing fis cal c oordination a nd i ntegration i n w ays that do n ot s urrender members' autonomy to make their own spending and tax decisions to a supra-EU ent ity. Rather, t he pr oposals s eek to stre ngthen c urrent Sta bility a nd Growth Pact rules, partly through some form of sanctions, and to provide more policy c oordination on budgets an d other fiscal m atters. Ba cked by t he €440 billion three- year EFSF fi nancing m echanism for Eurozone m embers and continued a ctive involvement of th e E CB in crisis management, Europ ean leaders may have a l imited peri od of t ime to ca lm financial m arkets a nd bolster confidence in the currency union.

Whether the currently contemplated reforms prove sufficient to ensure the sustainability and vi ability of th e c urrency uni on is unclear. A n umber of factors and developments could either bolster or destabilize the currency union in the years ahead.

Factors a nd developments tha t c ould b olster the E urozone include th e following:

- Given th at the EMU is largely a p olitical u ndertaking a nd a m ajor symbol of Eu ropean integration, Euro pean leaders and e lites m ay be highly motivated to keep the EMU intact.
- The pro posals under co nsideration i ntroduce i nstitutions and po licies that represent somewhat hi gher le vels of i ntegration and commitment to bu dgetary d iscipline – el ements that are considered necessary to rebuild market confidence in the euro for the future.
- The three-year period during whic h the EFSF will be in place gives European po licymakers tim e to d esign o ther measures to ha ndle any eventual sovereign default and to gain support for making the facility permanent.
- The EC B h as dem onstrated will ingness to help m embers in fisc al distress, and it has the tools to continue playing an active role in crisis management.
- The resc ue p rogram put i nto p lace basical ly overt urned the " no-bailout" ru le of the E MU, m aking st ates, at leas t in theory, mutually liable for the sovereign debt of fellow Eurozone members.
- The a cceptance by Eur opean pol icymakers of IMF involvem ent i n managing any future fiscal crises reinforces the fiscal insurance mechanism provided by the EFSF.

- Proposed reform s of labo r and pro duct markets in all Eur ozone countries, c ombined wi th stronger fiscal disc ipline, w ill improve the potential for economic growth and strengthen the euro in the long run.

Factors and possible developments that could weaken the sustainability of the currency union in its current form include the following:

- Partial sol utions proposed t o dat e create a moral hazard; if hea vily indebted countries think they will receive financial assistance from the EFSF, they may have few incentives to get their fiscal houses in order.
- A default or resched uling of G reek debt, w hich m any analy sts maintain is li kely, c ould p ose co ntagion effects on other h ighly-indebted Eurozone countries.
- In the e vent of a possib le sovere ign default or d efaults by Eurozone members, publi c su pport in s ome of the E urozone members for continued funding of the EFSF could decline.
- Fiscal m easures and shared responsi bility fo r d efaults co uld l ead to divisions am ong Euro zone members, causing som e members to reconsider the costs and benefits of membership.
- Persistent c urrent a ccount imbalances wi thin t he Eurozone, perhaps even more than the build-up of debt, can over the long-term become a challenge to the future stability of the Eurozone.
- The problem of current account imbalances may be complicated in the future by the proposed entry of mostly sm aller an d p oorer co untries into the EMU.
- Greater la bor mobility a nd wage f lexibility may not pre vent the accumulation of persistent economic imbalances that le d to the cris is and threaten the existence of the EMU.
- The f undamental problem of countries at v ery diff erent le vels of development living wit h a sin gle m onetary p olicy and a s ingle exchange rate will remain.

Table 2. Glossary of Terms

Term	Definition
Broad Economic Policy Guidelines (BEPG)	The *Broad Economic Policy Guidelines (BEPGs)* are adopted by the Council as a reference document guiding the conduct of the whole range of economic policies in the Member States and the European Union. They play a central role in the system of economic policy coordination, setting out economic policy recommendations which give a basis for economic policy in both the Member States and the EU as a whole in the current year.
Council of the European Union ("Council of Ministers" or "Council")	The *Council of the European Union* is the Union's main decision-making body and enacts legislation based on proposals from the European Commission. Its meetings are attended by the member state ministers, and is thus the institution which represents the member states. The Presidency of the Council rotates among the member states every six months.
Economic and Monetary Union (EMU)	*Economic and Monetary Union* (EMU) is the process of harmonizing the economic and monetary policies of the member states of the European Union with a view to the introduction of a single currency, the euro.
European Central Bank (ECB)	Founded on June 30, 1998, the *European Central Bank* (ECB) is the institution of the European Union responsible for setting the monetary policy of the 16 EU member states taking part in the Eurozone. The bank is headquartered in Frankfurt, Germany.
European Commission (EC)	*The European Commission* (EC) acts as the EU's executive branch, and has the right of legislative initiative. There are 27 Commissioners – one from each country.
European Council	The *European Council* brings together the leaders of the member states and the Commission President. It acts as a strategic guide and driving force for EU policy.
European Financial Stability Facility (EFSF)	The *European Financial Stability Facility* (EFSF) was set up by the 16 Eurozone countries to provide a funding backstop should a euro area Member State find itself in financial difficulties. The EFSF has the capacity to issue bonds guaranteed by euro area members for up to €440 billion in lending to Eurozone countries.
European Financial Stability Mechanism (EFSM)	The European Financial Stability Mechanism (EFSM) is a new €60 billion supranational EU balance of payments loan facility available to any EU member country facing financial difficulties.

Table 2. (Continued)

Term	Definition
The European System of Central Banks (ESCB)	The European System of Central Banks (ESCB) comprises the European Central Bank and the national central banks of all EU member states whether they have adopted the euro or not.
European Union (EU)	The *European Union* (EU) was established by the Treaty on European Union (Maastricht, 1992). The project of creating a Union has a long history, and was first mooted at the European Summit of 1972. The Union is both a political project and a form of legal organization.
Eurozone	The *Eurozone*, officially the *euro area*, is an economic and monetary union (EMU) of 16 EU members states which have adopted the euro currency as their sole legal tender. Monetary policy of the zone is the sole responsibility of the European Central Bank, though there is no common representation, governance or fiscal policy for the currency union. Some cooperation does, however, take place through the euro group, which makes political decisions regarding the Eurozone and the euro.
Excessive Deficit Procedure (EDP)	The excessive deficit procedure is governed by Article 104 of the Treaty establishing the European Community, under which member states are obliged to avoid excessive deficits in national budgets.
Lisbon Treaty	The *Lisbon Treaty*, the latest institutional reform treaty of the European Union (EU), went into effect on December 1, 2009. It seeks to give the EU a stronger and more coherent voice with the creation of a new position, President of the European Council. It also makes changes to the EU's internal decision-making mechanisms, and foreign policy apparatus, among other provisions.
Maastricht Treaty	*The Treaty of Maastricht,* formally, the *Treaty on European Union* (TEU), was signed on February 7, 1992 by members of the European Community in Maastricht, Netherlands. Upon its entry into force on November 1, 1993, it created the European Union and led to the creation of the single European currency, the euro.
Sovereign debt	Sovereign debt is a financial liability of a national government.
Stability and Growth Pact (SGP)	The *Stability and Growth Pact* (SGP) pertains to the third stage of economic and monetary union (EMU), which began on January 1,1999. It is intended to ensure that member states maintain budgetary discipline after the single currency has been introduced.

Source: Europa Glossary (http://europa.eu/scadplus/glossary/index-en.html).

ACKNOWLEDGMENTS

The au thors w ish to th ank the fol lowing CRS col leagues w ho pro vided helpful suggestions and comments on this report: Paul Belkin, Nils Bjorksten, William Cooper, Ian Fergusson, Marc Labonte, Derek Mix, and Dick Nanto.

End Notes

[1] For elaboration and analysis of the Greek debt crisis, see CRS Rep ort R41167, *Greece's Debt Crisis: Overview, Policy Responses, and Implications*, coordinated by Rebecca M. Nelson.

[2] Germany was widely criticized, including by U.S. officials, for waiting several months after the onset of the Gree k crisis in February 2010 before agreeing to loan fa cilities for Greec e and other Eurozone member states. German relu ctance is thought to have stemmed pr imarily from strong domestic opposition t o the proposed re lief packages. M any Germans consider Greece's problems to be a consequence of Greek go vernment profligacy and, as such , see Greece as a burd en on the German taxpayer. In light of this opposition, German Chan cellor Merkel insisted that the Greek government co mmit to significant austerity measures before giving her support to a European assistance p ackage. Nevertheless, th e significant German public opposition to assist ing Greece suggests th at the German gov ernment could have a difficult time winning support fo r future monetary transfers to oth er Eurozone cou ntries. This could present a significant cha llenge as European leaders engage in ongoing efforts to reform the architecture of the currency union, as well as shore up the banking sector.

[3] The U nited States is the large st financial contr ibutor to the IM F, and some Members of Congress have expressed reservations about the IMF loan to Greece. In response to the IMF loan to Greec e, Congress include d provisions in the financial regu latory legislation (P.L . 111-203) to protect IMF resources. For discu ssion and analysis of the role of the International Mo netary Fund, see CRS Re port R41239, *Frequently Asked Questions about IMF Involvement in the Eurozone Debt Crisis*, coordinated by Rebecca M. Nelson.

[4] A total of 16 s tates (A ustria, Belgium, C yprus, Finland, Franc e, Germany, Gre ece, Ireland, Italy, Luxembourg, Malta, Netherlands, Portugal, Slovakia, Spain, and Slovenia) of the 27-member European Union (EU) participate in an economic and monetary union (EMU) with the euro as the single currency. The other members of the EU are Bulgaria, Czech Republic, Denmark, Estonia, Hu ngary, Latv ia, Lithuani a, Pol and, Romania, S weden, and the United Kingdom. All 27 members take part in the "economic union" throu gh various forms of policy coordination, a single mark et, and single external trade policy, but 16 members have taken economic integration a step further, to the EMU. Denmark and the United Kingdom were granted special opt-outs of the currenc y union and are legally exempt from joining unless their governments decide otherwise, either by parliamentary vote or referendum. Sweden has gain ed a *de-facto* opt-out through the use of various legal provisions. All new members of the EU after 1994 need to adopt the euro as soon as they meet certain economic policy targets.

[5] Quoted in *Financial Times*, "Adrift Amid a Rift," by Ben Hall and Quentin Peel, June 24, 2010.

[6] For more infor mation, see H arold James, *International Monetary Cooperation Since Breton Woods* (Oxford: Oxford University Press, 1996).

[7] Katina Borsch, "Germany, The Euro and Politics of the B ail-out," *Centre for European Reform*, Briefing Note, June 2010.

[8] For further background on the e conomic costs and benefits of monetary union with a focus on the EMU, see Paul De Grouse, *Economics of Monetary Union* (Oxford: Oxford University Press, 2009).

[9] World Bank's World Development Indicators database. Data in current US$.

[10] World Bank's World Development Indicators database. Data in current US$.

[11] For more on t he bilateral econ omic relationshi p between the Uni ted States and th e EU, see CRS Rep ort RL 30608, *EU-U.S. Economic Ties: Framework, Scope, and Magnitude*, by William H. Cooper.

[12] Cost-in-freight data.

[13] U.S. Department of Commerce, Bureau of Economic Analysis, http://www.bea.gov.

[14] To participate in the initial formation of the EMU, each member had to meet the following five convergence criteria by 1998: (1   ) national legislation governing the country's fina ncial system had to be compatible with the treaty provisions controlling the European System of Central B anks; (2) a rate of inflation w ithin 1.5% of the rates in the three participating countries with th e lowest rates; (3) reduction of its government deficits to below 3% of its gross national p roduct; (4) currency exch ange ra tes within the limits defined by the Exchange Rate Mechanism (ERM) (an intermed iary step toward a single currency that attempted to stabilize exchange rates by fixing rates through variable bands) for at least two years; and (5)inte rest rates within 2% of the rates in the three partic ipating countries with the lowest rates.

[15] Paul De Grouse, *Economics of Monetary Union.*

[16] Article 125 TFEU is often referred to as the EU's "no-bailout" clause. It states:
The Union shall not be liable for or assume the commitments of   central governments, regional, local or other public authorities, other bodies governed by public law, or p ublic undertakings of a ny Member State, without pre judice to mutual finan cial guarantees for the joint execution of a specific projec t. A Member State shall not be liable for or assume the commitments of central governments, regional, local or other public authorities,   other bodies governed by public law, or public undertak ings of another Member State, without prejudice to mutual financial guarantees for the joint execution of a specific project.

[17] European leaders drew referen ce to these exc eptions (Article 122 (2) TFE U) in crafting new crisis management facilit ies. They explicitly based the bailout actions on the grounds that the debt crisis endangered the solvency of entire states and posed a serious threat to the euro and financial sta bility of the mo netary union. For a contrary view   that the euro w   as endangered by t he crisis, see Hans-Werner Sinn, "Rescuing   Europe," *CWSifo Forum*, Volume 1, August 2010. Sinn argues that the bailout was en gineered primarily to protect French, and to a lesser extent, German banks.

[18] The Protocol on Excessive Deficit Procedure es tablished a mechanism for countrie s to meet the specific guidelines that are applied under   Article 104 of the Ma astricht Treaty. Unde r this protocol, EU members are expected to have an annual budget deficit no greater than 3% of GDP at market prices and government debt no more than an amount equivalent to 60% of GDP.

[19] The Stability and Growth Pact (SGP) is an agreement by European Union members to conduct their fiscal policy in a manner that facilitates and maintains the EMU. The Pact is based on Articles 99 and 104 of the Maas tricht Treaty, a nd related decisions. It consists of (1) a political com mitment by all pa   rties involved i n the SGP to the full and   timely implementation of the budget surveillance pro   cess; (2) regular   surveillance ai med at preventing budge t deficits from going above   the 3 % reference valu e; and (3) correc tive elements w hich r equire member states to   take immediate action when the 3%   reference value is breached or face the imposition of sanctions.

[20] Beetsma, Roel M.W .J., and Xa vier Debrun , *Implementing the Stability and Growth Pact: Enforcement and Procedural Flexibility*, IMF W orking Paper W P/05/59, International Monetary Fund, March 2005.

[21] Martin Feldstein, "The Euro's Fundamental Flaws," *The International Economy*, Spring 2010, p. 11.

[22] Faltin, Dirk, and Katherine Klingensmith, "Euro zone Economics: The Future of t he Euro in Jeopardy," *UBS Wealth Management Research*, July 13, 2010.

[23] Martin Feldstein, p.12.

[24] B ank for Int ernational Settle ments (B IS), *International Banking and Financial Market Developments*, BIS Quarte rly Review, June 2010, http://www.bi s.org/publ/ qtrpdf/r_qt1006.pdf.

[25] Bank for International Settlements (BIS), "Consolidated International Claims of BIS Reporting Banks," Publication data up to 2009Q4, June 2010, Table 9B: Consolidated Foreign Claims of R eporting Banks - Immediate B orrower B asis, http://w ww.bis.org/ st atistics/ consstats.htm.

[26] Gilles Saint-Paul, "Is the Euro a Failure?", *VoxEU*, May 5, 2010.

[27] Uri Da dush a nd Bennett Stan cil, "Europe's Debt C risis: More than a Fiscal Problem, " in *Paradigm Lost: The Euro in Crisis*, ed. Uri Dadush and Contributors (Carnegie Endowment for International Peace, 2010), pp. 9-15.

[28] The current account is the sum of the balance of trade (exports minus imports of g oods and services), net fa ctor income suc h as intere st pay ments and divid ends, and net transfer payments such as foreign aid. Measures to reduce a current account deficit usually inv olve increasing exports or decreasing imports. Economists tend to argue that this ca n be accomplished most effectively by increasing dom estic savings or re ducing borrowin g of households and government.

[29] Dirk F altin and Katherine Klingensmith, "Euroz one Ec onomics: The Future of th e Euro i n Jeopardy," p. 6.

[30] Given that about 75% of al l Eurozone trade constitutes exports o f one Eurozone member to another (so-called "intra-Eurozone trade"), the tra de surpluses of one Eurozone co untry or group of countries are to a large extent matched by the deficits of others.

[31] Gilles Saint-Paul, "Is the Euro a Failure?", *VoxEU*, May 5, 2010.

[32] D ick Faltin and K atherine Klingensmith, "Euroz one Economics: The Futu re of the Euro In Jeopardy," p.5.

[33] Ibid., p. 8.

[34] IMF, "Frequently Asked Questions: Greece," May 11, 2010 , http://www.imf.org/external/ np/exr/ faq/greecefaqs.htm.

[35] The c urrent balance of payment s facility wa s created under Article 143 of the Lisb on Treaty, which limits ass istance to "member states w ith a derogation, " i.e. , those outside the Eurozone.

[36] Council Re gulation (EU) No . 407/2010 of 11 May 2010 establ ishing a Euro pean financial stabilization mec hanism. Official Journal of the European Union , December 5 , 20 10. L 118/1.

[37] Council of the European Union, Press Release, Extraordinary Council Meeting, Economic and Financial Affairs, Brussels, May 9/10, 2010.

[38] Deutsche Bank Research , "E uropean Governance: What does the future holds,? August 6, 2010. Moral haz ard is a term that refers to situations when a party insulated from ris k behaves differently than it would behave if it were fully exposed to the risk.

[39] Ibid.

[40] David Oakley , Peter Garnham, and Ralph Atkin, "E CB reveals €16.5bn bond p urchases," *Financial Times*, May 17, 2010.

[41] Andrew Ross Sorkin, "ECB Winds Down Debt Purchases," *New York Times*, July 20, 2010.

[42] In response to the beginnings of the recent financial crisis, similar s wap lines were established in December 2007 and expired in February 2010. On the re-establishment of these lines, see Federal Reserve , "Federal Reserv e, Euro pean Cen tral Bank, Ba nk of Canada , Ba nk of England, an d Swiss National Bank Announc e Re establishment of Temporary U.S. Dollar Liquidity Sw ap Facilit ies," *http://www.federalreserve.gov/newsevents/press/*

monetary/20100509a.htm and   Federal Reserve, " FOMC Authorizes Re-establishment of Temporary U.S. Dollar Liquidity Swap   Arrangement w ith the B   ank of Japan," http://www.federalreserve.gov/newsevents/press/monetary/20100510a.htm.

[43] Europea n Co uncil, *European Council, Conclusions, 17 June 2010*, E UCO 13/10, Brussels, June 17, 2010.

[44] Simon Taylor, "Germany to push nine financial reforms," *EuropeanVoice.com*, May 21, 2010. Adam Cohen, "EU Needs Permanent Crisis-Resolution Fund," *Dow Jones*, April 14, 2010.

[45] According to the authors of the proposal, EU countries should pool up to 60% of GDP of their national debt as s enior sovereign debt, there by reducing the borrowing cost for tha t part of the debt (blue bonds). Any national debt beyond a country's Blue Bond allocation should be issued as national debt, junior to b lue bonds, with s ound proced ures for an orderly de fault (Red Bonds). Ja cques Delphla a nd Jakob von   Weizsacker, *The Blue Bond Proposal*, Breugel, Brussels, May 10.

[46] International Monetary Fund, *Euro Area Policies: 2010 Article IV Consultation*, Washington, DC, July 2010.

[47] Lorenzo Bini Smaghi, *Imbalances and Sustainability in the Euro Area*, Europe an Central Bank, Presentation at the ECB and its Watchers Conference, Frankfurt, July 9, 2010.

[48] Michael Pettis, "The R isk of Another G lobal Trade War," *Financial Times,* August 24, 2010 , p. 9.

[49] Christian Riermann, " How Germany's Export Strength Helps Its Neighbors," *Spiegel Online,* August 24, 2010.

[50] Jack Ewing, "Merkel Urges Tougher Rules for Euro Zone," *New York Times*, March 17, 2010.

[51] Barry Eichen green, "The Eur   o: Love It or   Leave It ?," *VoxEU*, No vember 17, 2007 , http://www.voxeu.org/index.php?q=node/729.

[52] Mark Cliffe, Maarten Leen, an d Peter Vanden Houte, et al., *EMU Break-up: Quantifying the Unthinkable*, ING Financial Markets Research, June 7, 2010, p. 8.

[53] Gerard Baker, "Will Germany Leave the Euro?," *The Spectator*, June 19, 2010, pp. 14-15.

[54] Ibid.

[55] Wolgang Proissi, "Why Germany Fell Out of Love with Europe," *Brueghel Essay and Lecture Series,* July 2020, pp.15-17.

[56] At the same time, the value of northern banks' euro-denominated assets would still fall relative to their liabilities denominated in new currency.

[57] Peter Boockvar, "Greece Will Have To Restructure: Equity Strategist," *CNBC*, June 28, 2010.

[58] Daniel Gros, "Are the Barbarians a the EU's Gates?" *Europeanvoice.com*, May 25, 2010.

[59] Zsolt D arvas, "Fiscal Federalism in C risis: Lessons for Europe from the U S," *Bruegel Policy Contribution,* Issue 2010/07, July 2010.

[60] The euro, for example, has depr eciated by 15% against the dollar between December 12, 2009 and August 13, 2010 (from 1.51 $/€ to 1.28$/€).

[61] Fred B ergsten, "New Imbalances Will Threaten Global Recovery," *Financial Times,* June 10, 2010.

[62] Jeremy J. Siegel, "Upside of the Euro Crisis," Kiplinger's Personal Finance, July 5. 2010.

[63] ING Global Economics, "EMU Break-up: Quantifying the Unthinkable," July 7, 2010.

[64] Desmond Lachman, "Euro Will Unravel, and Soon," *American Enterprise Institute for Public Policy Research,* No. 2, September 2010.

[65] BBC Business News, "Eurozone growth of 1% confirmed," September 2, 2010.

[66] Website: [ht tp://clinton6.nara.gov/1999/01/1999-01-04-statement-by-the -president - on- the launch - of- the- euro.html]

In: The Eurozone: Testing the Monetary Union   ISBN: 978-1-61209-113-6
Editors: H.J. Farkas and D.C. Murphy   © 2011 Nova Science Publishers, Inc.

Chapter 2

FREQUENTLY ASKED QUESTIONS ABOUT IMF INVOLVEMENT IN THE EUROZONE DEBT CRISIS*

Rebecca M. Nelson, Dick K. Nanto, Jonathan E. Sanford and Martin A. Weiss

SUMMARY

On May 2, 2010, the E urozone m ember stat es a nd the Int ernational Monetary Fund (IMF) a nnounced an unprecedented €110 bi llion (about $145 billion) financial assistance package for G reece. The following week, on May 9, 2 010, EU leaders an nounced th at t hey w ould m ake an a dditional €500 billion (a bout $63 6 b illion) in fina ncial assista nce a vailable t o v ulnerable European co untries, and su ggested that t he IMF cou ld co ntribute up t o an additional €220 b illion t o €250 bi llion (about $ 280 b illion to $318 bil lion). This re port answers frequently asked questions about IMF involvement in the Eurozone debt crisis.

---

* This is an e dited, reformatted and augmented version of Co ngressional Researc h Service publication, Report R41239, dated August 27, 2010.

For more information on the Greek de bt crisis, see CRS Report R41167, *Greece's Debt Crisis: Overview, Policy Responses, and Implications*, coordinated by Rebecca M. Nelson.

BACKGROUND ON THE EUROZONE AND THE IMF

What is the Eurozone?

The Eurozone refers to t he group of E uropean Union (EU) countries that use the euro (€) as their national currency. The euro was introduced in 1999 as an accounting currency and i n 2002 as ph ysical currency in circulation. The Eurozone or iginally included 11 co untries a nd h as since e xpanded to 16 countries. Greece joined the Eurozone in 2000. Currently, the c ountries in the Eurozone i nclude Austr ia, Bel gium, C yprus, Finland, France, Germ any, Greece, Irela nd, Ita ly, Luxem bourg, Malta, t he Netherlands, Portuga l, Slovakia, Slovenia, and Spain.

The EU has 27 m ember states . Denm ark, Sweden, a nd the United Kingdom are members of the EU that have opted out of joining the Eurozone. All recent entrants to the EU, including Bulgaria, the Czech Republic, Estonia, Hungary, L atvia, Lit huania, Pola nd, an d Rom ania, ar e req uired to adopt the euro as their national currency as soon as poss ible, but m ust meet certa in economic policy targets before they are eligible. Budgetary discipline is one of the criteria f or jo ining t he eur o. Un der the Tre aty on E uropean Uni on, commonly referred to as the Maastricht Treaty, EU member states are required to stay below a gov ernment budget deficit ceiling of 3% of G DP and external debt ceiling of 60% of G DP. Enforcem ent by EU authorities has been weak, however, and many governments have exceeded these ceilings. When the euro was introduced, some raised concerns about the viability of an economic union that has a common monetary policy but diverse national fiscal policies.

What is the IMF?

The In ternational M onetary Fund (IM F) is an i nternational fi nancial institution that was created after World War II to prom ote exchange rate and monetary sta bility. Th e fou nders aim ed to a void t he be ggar-thy-neighbor exchange rat e poli cies and banking i nstability t hat d eepened th e De pression during t he 1930s a nd the lack of any i nternational mechanism for sett ing standards or coordinating policy. The IMF has changed over time as the world financial sy stem has e volved. I t n ow provides more t echnical assistance to member coun tries on banking a nd f inance issu es. However, its prin cipal function is s till o ne of lending m oney and e ncouraging ref orm to h elp countries d eal with ba lance-of-payments and fina ncial crises. T he m ain concern is the possible contagion effects that might bring down other countries if a crisis in a specific country is not addressed.

The IMF is owned by its member countries, whose votes are proportional to the amount óf money they have subscribed to help fund its operations. The IMF funds i ts ow n internal bu dget fro m in come earn ed through its le nding program. The disb ursements for IMF lo ans are generally co nditional o n t he borrower country im plementing reform s. Loans are gen erally dis bursed i n phases ("tranches") in order to enc ourage compliance with loan conditions. If conditions are not met, funds are not disbursed. The IMF charges its borrowers a rate of int erest roug hly equ ivalent t o the pric e th at major gov ernments around t he w orld p ay to b orrow funds, and i t p ays its member cou ntries interest when it uses their quota resources to fund its loans. Disbursements for its re gular l oans, c alled Sta nd-By A rrangements (SBA), are re payable i n fi ve to eight years. Repayments for some of the IMF's m ore specialized programs may occur over a l onger period of t ime. U ntil t he mid-1970s, developed countries were frequent borrowers from the IMF. Since t hen, d eveloping countries (par ticularly em erging m arkets) have been the princ ipal b orrowers. However, during t he re cent fin ancial cr isis, the IMF le nt s ubstantially to several of the new er m embers of t he E uropean U nion (EU), and it has a lso assisted countries with advanced economies from time to time.

EUROZONE/IMF FINANCIAL ASSISTANCE PACKAGE FOR GREECE

Why Did Greece Turn to the other Eurozone Member States and the IMF for Financial Assistance?

Over the past dec ade, Gre ece borrowed hea vily in international c apital markets to f und go vernment budget a nd tra de deficits. H igh government spending, w eak r evenue co llection, struc tural r igidities, a nd loss of competitiveness are typic ally cit ed a s major factors behind Greece's accumulation of debt. Access to capital at low interest rates after adopting the euro and weak enforcement of EU rules concerning debt and deficit ceilings may also have played a role.

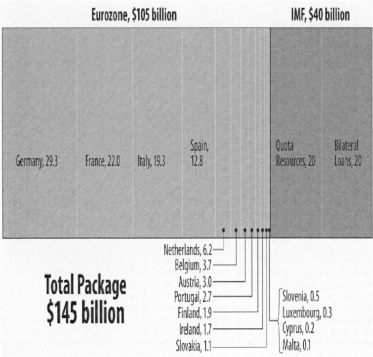

Source: Graphic prepared b y CRS using da ta from Jan Strupczewski, "Factbox - Progress Towards Approving Emergency Loans to Greece," *Reuters*, May 6, 2010 ; and IMF, "Frequently A sked Questions: Greece ," M ay 11 , 2010, *http://www.imf.org/ external/np/exr/faq/greecefaqs.htm#q23.*

Notes: Eurozone member state commitments are bilateral loans, and some commitments are subject to par liamentary appro val. IMF quota resources and bilateral loans fund a Stand-By Arrangement (SBA) loan for Greece. Conversion to dollars from euros using exchange rate of €1= $1.318.

Figure 1. Eurozone/IMF Financial Assistance Package for Greece Eurozone member state or IMF source of resources, Billion US$.

Reliance on financing fro m interna tional c apital m arkets l eft Gr eece highly vulne rable t o shi fts in in vestor confi dence. Inves tors becam e increasingly nervous in October 20 09, wh en th e n ewly elected Greek government nearly doubled the government 2009 budget deficit estimate. Over the n ext months, t he g overnment an nounced severa l auster ity pac kages a nd had suc cessful rou nds of b ond sal es o n international capital markets to ra ise needed funds. In late April 2010, when the European Union's (EU's) statistical agency, Eur ostat, f urther revised t he estimate of Greece's 2009 def icit upwards, G reek bond spre ads s piked a nd tw o m ajor credi t ra ting agencies downgraded Greek bonds. Greece's de bt cris is threatened t o sprea d to ot her European c ountries, i ncluding Irel and, It aly, Portu gal, an d Spa in, t hat m ay face fiscal challenges similar to Greece.

The Greek government formally requested financial assistance from the 16 countries that use the e uro as the ir nat ional c urrency (the E urozone) and t he IMF on A pril 23, 2 010. It was hope d that the fina ncial assist ance, combined with aus terity measures, would pr event the Greek governm ent from restructuring or defaulting on its debt or, more dram atically, from aband oning the euro in favor of a national currency.

What Financial Assistance is being Provided to Greece?

On May 2, 20 10, the Eur ozone m ember states a nd the IMF anno unced a three-year, €110 billion (about $1 45 bil lion) financial assista nce pac kage for Greece.[1] This pac kage t akes the f orm of loa ns m ade at market-based int erest rates.

Figure 1 sh ows the so urces o f fu nds for the fi nancial assistance package for Greece. Eurozone countr ies are to contribut e €80 bi llion (ab out $105 billion) in bilateral loans. Each of the Eurozone countries (besides Greece) has pledged a b ilateral loan, wit h the largest bilateral l oans ple dged by Germany and France (about $29.3 billion and $22 billion, respectively).

The IMF is to contribut e a €30 bil lion (abo ut $ 40 b illion) l oan.[2] Of the total, th e IM F w ould dra w half from IMF qu ota re sources (th e financial commitment countries make to the IMF upon j oining) and half from bil ateral lines of credit pledged by some member countries.

It is worth n oting that it is not c lear how m uch of the €1 10 billion (about $145 billion) committed by the IMF a nd the Eurozone member states will be used by Greec e. The money is disbur sed in phases as Greece meets IMF loan conditions. If IMF officials say that Greece does not meet these c onditions, IMF dis bursements w ill n ot be m ade. A lternatively, if cred itor c onfidence i n Greece is restored a nd Gr eece ca n res ume selling bonds on int ernational capital m arkets at reasona ble i nterest ra tes, t he Gree k governm ent may not need to rely on Eurozone and IMF financial commitments. On the other hand, some economists have predicted that the financial package for Greece may not be suffi cient to pre vent Gre ece from rest ructuring i ts debt and/or exi ting t he Eurozone.

What is the U.S. Contribution to the IMF Loan to Greece?

The IMF loan t o G reece is to be fin anced by tw o d ifferent s ources of money. Half of the IMF loan to Greece (about $20 billion) will be financed by IMF quot a resources. IMF quot as are the fina ncial c ommitments that IMF members make upon joining the IMF and are broadly bas ed o n the IMF member's relati ve siz e in t he w orld e conomy. The U .S. contr ibution to IMF quota reso urces is 17%. H owever, we cannot infer that 17% of th e IMF loan financed by IMF quota resources (about $20 billion) is from the United States. Once the IMF Executi ve Board a pproves a spe cific loan, t here is an administrative decision made by the IMF as to which countries' quotas will be tapped t o fund t hat part icular l oan. Th e IM F d oes no t di sclose part ies on individual transactions, but over t ime aim s to provid e a bal anced position for all members.

The other half (about $20 billion) of the IMF loan to Greece is expected to be fin anced by bilat eral l oans. Thes e bi lateral l oans will be come part of th e IMF's supp lemental fu nd, the New A rrangements to Bo rrow (NAB), wh en it becomes operati onal. They are a vailable now, however, before the e xpanded NAB goes into effect. I n 2009, the United States e nacted legislation to extend a l ine of cred it w orth $100 bi llion as part of ex panding the N AB. However, because t he expanded N AB is not y et operational, t his $100 b illion line of credit from the United States cannot be tapped for Greece's package.

The United States has never lost money on its commitment to the IMF. All U.S. financial interactions with th e I MF are off-budget and, becaus e of accounting factors, do not r esult in any net outlays or have any impact on the U.S. federal budget deficit.

What is the IMF's Creditor Status in its Loan to Greece?

The IMF, li ke the other in ternational fin ancial i nstitutions, en joys a de facto preferred creditor status ; member go vernments gra nt priority to repayment of their ob ligations to the IMF over other creditors. In the case of the Gree ce loan, IMF l oans would be repai d prior to all ot her credi tors.

Financing from European c ountries will be junior to the IMF's loa n and will have the same status as existing Greek debt.

Who Bears the Risk of the IMF's Loan to Greece?

The IMF's membership as a whole bears any risk from lending to Greece, but, in i ts entire history, no member of t he IMF has e xperienced a loss fro m providing resources to the IMF, either by lending to the IMF or thr ough the payment of quota su bscriptions. Furthermore, member countries whose q uota resources are chose n for a spec ific IM F loan have a claim on the IMF's balance shee t as a whole. Thus, e ven if U.S. quota is drawn for th e Greece loan, which may be likely, any associated risk to t he IMF's balance sheet due to the IMF loan to Greece would be shared by all IMF members. The IMF has preferred cre ditor stat us, which m eans tha t th e IMF, al ong with o ther international financial institutions, is first in line to get repaid by the member country, ahead of other creditors. Occasionally countries fall into arrears with the IMF, but no member country has lost money as a result.

What Reforms are Part of Greece's Package with the IMF?

The IMF do es not disburse the full amount of its l oans to governments at once. Instead, the IMF wil l divide the l oan into tranches (French for "slice") and wi ll o nly disb urse th e nex t tran che after verify ing t hat the spec ified economic pol icy reform s have been m et. U rging policy reform s in th is w ay ensures th at the lo ans wi ll be rep aid to th e IM F, and th at th e re quired economic reforms are implemented.

The IMF pr ogram for Greece c alls for substa ntial reduc tions in government spending as well as revenue increases. Overall, the package aims to reduce Gre ece's government budget de ficit from 13.6% of GDP in 2009 to below 3 % of G DP by 20 14. Th e IMF has referred to t his program as unprecedented in term s of the ad justment effort require d by the government.[3] Some of the key reforms included in Greece's program with the IMF are listed below.

In the en d, IMF invo lvement w as repor tedly a key con dition of G erman Chancellor M erkel's wil lingness t o pr ovide fi nancial assistance to Greece. Some argue that the p olicy reform s (condit ionality) at tached to an I MF loa n would le nd additional impetus t o ref orm and pro vide b oth t he G reek government and t he EU w ith an   outside sca pegoat for pushi ng throu gh politically unpopular reforms.

KEY ELEMENTS OF THE GREECE'S REFORM PACKAGE WITH THE IMF

- **Government revenues.** Re venue m easures are to yi eld 4% of GD P through 2013 by raising the value-added tax and taxes on luxury items, tobacco, and alcohol, among other items.
- **Revenue administration and expenditure control.** T he Greek government is to s trengthen its tax co llection a nd raise co ntributions from those w ho have not carried a fair share of th e tax burden. It is to safeguard rev enue from the larges t ta x p ayers and s trengthen b udget controls. Th e total revenu e gains and ex penditure savi ngs fro m t hese structural reforms are expec ted to gradually total 1.8% of GDP during the program period.
- **Financial stability.** A Fin ancial Sta bility Fund, fun ded from the external fi nancing pac kage, is bein g set up to ensure a sound le vel of bank equity.
- **Entitlement programs.** Government e ntitlement pro grams are to   be curtailed; se lected soc ial secur ity be nefits are t o be cu t whi le maintaining benefits for the most vulnerable.
- **Pension reform.** C omprehensive p ension reform is prop osed, including by curtailing provisions for early retirement.
- **Structural policies.** Government to m odernize pu blic adm inistration, strengthen labor markets an d i ncome pol icies, im prove th e b usiness environment, and divest state enterprises.
- **Cut military spending.** The p lan envisages a si gnificant red uction in military expenditure during the period.

Source: IMF, "Europe and IMF Agree €110 Billion Financing Plan W ith Greece," May 2, 2010, /www.i   mf.org/external/pubs/ft/survey/ so/20 10/car 050210 a. htm..

The EU would also make policy reforms a condition of loans, but the IMF is seen as more independent than the EU and has more experience in resolving debt crises than the EU. Some have also argued that IMF participation also reportedly enabled Eurozone countries to agree more easily on the terms and conditions of the loan program than might have been the case had they had to arrange it separately.

What is Unusual about the Greece Package with the IMF?

On the one hand, the IMF loan to Greece is a standard IMF program. The IMF lends to countries facing balance-of-payment difficulties, and it is widely agreed that Greece was facing substantial balance-of-payments problems. Greece, as a member of the IMF, is entitled to draw on IMF resources, pending approval by the IMF management. The procedure by which Greece obtained its loan from the IMF was standard, as was the specific IMF loan instrument to Greece (a three-year Stand-By Arrangement [SBA]).

On the other hand, Greece's program with the IMF is unusual for two reasons. First, since the late 1970s, the IMF has not generally lent to developed countries and has never lent to a Eurozone member state since the euro was created. That said, the IMF has had programs with countries in Europe before but, with the exception of Iceland's IMF program in 2008, IMF involvement in Europe has not been recent. For example, in the 1970s, the IMF had programs with the United Kingdom, Spain, and Italy. In the early 1980s, the IMF also had a program with Portugal.

Second, Greece's program with the IMF is unusual for its relative magnitude. The IMF has general limits on the amount it will lend to a country either through an SBA or Extended Fund Facility (EFF), which is similar to an SBA but for countries facing longer-term balance-of-payments problems. The IMF's guidelines for limits on the size of loans for SBAs and EFFs are 200% of a member's quota annually and 600% of a member's quota cumulatively.[4] IMF quotas are the financial commitments that IMF members make upon joining the IMF and are broadly based on the IMF member's relative size in the world economy. In "exceptional" situations, the IMF reserves the right to lend in excess of these limits, and has done so in the past. The IMF's loan to Greece is indeed exceptional access at 3,200% of Greece's IMF quota and is the largest access of IMF quota resources granted to an IMF member country.[5] Previously, the largest access had been granted to South Korea during the

Asian fi nancial cr isis in t he 1990s, a t ne arly 2, 000% of K orea's qu ota resources.

What other Policy Options Did Greece have?

Greece is a ddressing its s overeign de bt crisis through a   mix of fisca l austerity measures and structural reforms to improve the competitiveness of its industries. M any bel ieve t hat t he m easures bei ng im plemented by t he G reek government will l   ead to low le vels of ec onomic growt h a nd in crease unemployment. Fina ncial assistance from the other Euroz one member states and the IMF i s allowing the adjustment to take place o ver a lon ger pe riod o f time.

Greece c ould have addressed its soverei gn debt crisis by restructuring its debt or by le aving t he E urozone. So me econom ists belie ve t hat Gre ece m ay still be forced to pursue one or both of these policy options. Debt restructuring, for exam ple by neg otiating w ith its bond holders t o ext end t he maturity of Greek bonds or to ta ke a cut in debt re payments, would alleviate i mmediate pressure on   the G   reek gover nment's debt pay   ments. H owever, d ebt restructuring could a ccelerate t he c ontagion of t he c risis to o ther Eurozone countries, as well as hinder Greece's ability to regain access to capital markets in the future.

Greece c ould also have addressed i ts so vereign debt cr isis by l eaving the Eurozone. Th is w ould req uire aba ndoning th e eur o, is suing a n ew nat ional currency, and al lowing the n ew national cu rrency t o depreciate against the euro. The Greek go vernment would also prob ably hav e to p ut restrictions on bank withdrawals to pre vent a run o n the banks during the tr ansition from the euro to a national currency. It is thought by some that a new national currency depreciated a gainst the euro woul d s pur export-led growth in   Greece and offset the c ontractionary effects of fi scal aust erity. Since Greece 's debt i s denominated in euros, however, leaving the Eurozone in favor of a depreciated national c urrency would rai se the value of Greece's de bt in terms of na tional currency an d put press   ure on ot   her vul nerable Europe an   countries. Additionally, some argue that a G reek de parture from the E urozone would be economically catastr ophic, lead t o c ontagion t o ot her Eu ropean countries facing sim ilar circum stances, a nd have serious ram ifications for   political relations among the European states and future European integration.

EUROZONE/IMF FINANCIAL ASSISTANCE PACKAGE
FOR OTHER EUROZONE COUNTRIES

Why Did the Eurozone Leaders Pledge Support to other Eurozone Countries?

Despite t he enactment of the E urozone/IMF assistance pac kage for Greece, investor concerns about the sustainability of E urozone debt deepened during the first week of May 2010. Driven down by such fears, global stock markets plunged sharply on May 6, 2010, and the euro fell to a 15-month low against the dollar. Seeking to head off the possibility of contagion to countries such as Portugal and Spain, EU finance ministers agreed on May 9, 2010, to a broader €500 bi llion (ab out $636 b illion) fi nancial assist ance package available to vulnerable Eurozone governments. Some analysts assert that such a bold, large-scale move had become an urgent imperative for the EU in order to break t he momentum of a gathering European fi nancial crisis. Inves tors initially reac ted p ositively to t he announcement of th e new a greement, wit h global stock markets rebounding on May 10, 2010, to regain the sharp losses of the week before.

What Financial Assistance Has been Pledged by the EU and the IMF?

The bulk of assistance is to be provided through a new European Financial Stability Facility (EFSF). T he facility, which expires after three years, raises funds by selling bo nds an d other debt instruments, ba cked by gu arantees of Eurozone member states, on inter national capital markets. The EFSF can provide up to €440 billion (about $560 bi llion) in l oans to E urozone member states.

EU l eaders al so an nounced th e creation of a new supran ational EU balance of payments loan facili ty available to a ny EU m ember country facing financial difficulties. T his facility, c alled t he Euro pean Fi nancial Stability Mechanism (EFSM) raises funds on international capital markets using the EU budget as collateral. T he E FSM can provide up to €60 billion (ab out $ 76 billion) in loans to EU members. The EFSM is sim ilar in design to an existing €50 billion EU balance of payments facility that can only be drawn on by non-

Eurozone EU member nations, including Latvia, Hungary, and Romania. No country to date has drawn on the EFSF or the EFSM.

EU leaders also suggested the IMF could contribute up to an additional €220 billion to €250 billion (about $280 billion to about $318 billion). This is in line with the Greece package, where the Eurozone states contributed roughly two-thirds and the IMF one-third of the total. IMF Deputy Managing Director John Lipsky reportedly later clarified the news reports about the IMF contribution to broader Eurozone stabilization efforts, saying that these pledges were "illustrative" of the support that the IMF could provide.[6] Reportedly, Lipsky reiterated that the IMF only provides loans to countries that have requested IMF assistance and that Greece is the only Eurozone country to date that has requested IMF assistance.[7]

Finally, the European Central Bank (ECB) also announced it would buy member state bonds in order to increase market confidence. This is an activity in which it had not previously engaged, and some view this action as a compromise to the central bank's independence. As of July 20, 2010, the ECB held around €60 billion of European government bonds.[8]

What is the Role of the U.S. Federal Reserve?[9]

On May 9, 2010, the Federal Reserve (Fed) announced the re-establishment of temporary reciprocal currency agreements, known as swap lines, with the European Central Bank, Bank of Canada, the Bank of England, Bank of Japan, and the Swiss National Bank.[10] These arrangements have been authorized through January 2011.

Under these agreements the Fed swaps dollars for foreign currencies for a fixed period of time with interest being paid to the Fed on the dollar amounts involved. The swaps are repaid at the exchange rate at the time of the original swap, meaning that these repayment amounts are not affected by changes in exchange rates while the swap is outstanding. Thus, there is no exchange rate risk and, except in the unlikely event that the borrowing country's currency becomes unconvertible in foreign exchange markets, there is also no credit risk involved for the Fed. The highest recent outstanding amount was approximately $583 billion in December 2008.

The swap lines are intended to provide liquidity to banks in non-domestic denominations. For example, many European banks have borrowed in dollars to finance dollar-denominated transactions, such as the purchase of U.S. assets. Normally, foreign banks could finance their dollar-denominated borrowing through the private inter-bank lending market. Such private lending markets, however, have greatly diminished, if no t disappeared, in periods of crisis over the past few years. Thus, central banks at home and abroad have taken a m uch larger rol e in dire ctly pro viding li quidity to ba nks. The swa p lines with the Federal Reserve provide foreign central banks with a source of dollar liquidity should such liquidity be needed.

IMF RESOURCES AND CONGRESS'S ROLE

How Much Money does the IMF Have to Lend?

In A pril 20 09, th e G -20 Lead ers and the Int ernational M onetary and Financial Comm ittee agre ed t o increas e the res ources ava ilable t o the IMF through im mediate bi lateral fi nancing from members and t o su bsequently expand the N AB and m ake it m ore flexi ble.[11] Res ources fro m new bil ateral contributions are available and being drawn on for current IMF programs. The expanded NAB is not yet operational.

As of July 15, 2010, the IMF has about $225.5 billion dollars immediately available to l end.[12] This fi gure is the I MF's one -year forward commit ment capacity (FCC), w hich m easures th e IMF's abili ty to make new non-concessional r esources a vailable t o m embers over the next 1 2 m onths. Th is includes, am ong ot her so urces, u nused quo ta reso urces, curren tly activ e bilateral l oans to the IM F fro m several a dvanced eco nomies, and n ote purchase agreements with three large emerging-market countries.[13]

What is the Expanded New Arrangements to Borrow (NAB)?

Created in t he late 1 990s, the New Arra ngements to Borrow (NA B) is a supplemental fund th at th e IMF can use to finance lo ans under ex ceptional circumstances that pose a threat to the international monetary system. The G-20 proposed in April 2009 that the existing NAB be exp anded and made more flexible in li ght of in creased demand for IMF assistance. Following a year of negotiations on t he d esign and operations of th e ex panded N AB, the IMF Executive Board ad opted a prop osal o n April 1 2, 2010, by w hich the N AB would b e e xpanded t o about $ 550 billion, w ith the ad dition of 13 new participating countries.[14] The U.S. co mmitment to t he expanded NAB is $100 billion a nd th e ne cessary a uthorizations and appropriations w ere e nacted i n FY2009.[15]

Despite U .S. appro val of its con   tribution to t he e xpanded N AB i n FY2009, the expanded NAB is not y et operational and U.S. resources pledged to it cannot be activated until a s ufficient num ber of curre nt and new participants p rovide form al cons ent. Pa rticipating i n the   expanded N AB involves d omestic appro val pro cedures in   many coun tries, including legislative approval before they can consent or a dhere to t he expanded NAB. The IMF has not published the status of NAB appro vals. Once the expanded NAB becom es operat ional, the bi lateral loan and note purchas e agr eements would be folded into the NAB.

If and whe n the e xpanded NAB be comes operat ional, t he process for approving use of NAB resources will   change. Under t he current NAB, NAB resources c an be used if   approval is secure d fro m: (1) N AB partici pants representing 8 0% of to tal NAB credit arrangements; and (2) members of the IMF Exec utive Board repr esenting 50% of the vot ing share . Use of NAB resources is c urrently cons idered on a loan-by-loan ba sis. Under the current NAB, the U nited St ates d oes not h ave suf ficient voting power to unilaterally veto use of NAB resources.

Under t he e xpanded N AB, the N AB w ould be a ctivated for a period of time (up to si x months). During this "activation period," calls can be made on the NAB wit hout a dditional c onsent by the NAB p articipants or the IMF Executive Board. To activate the expanded NAB, it will be necessary to secure approval fro m: (1) NAB participants represe nting 85% of to tal N AB credit arrangements eli gible to vot e; and (2) m embers of the IMF Exec utive Boar d representing 50% of the voting share. Under the expanded and modified NAB, the Uni ted States will b e able to un ilaterally vet o act ivating the N AB. If the expanded and modified NAB is acti vated, however, the United States will not be a ble to dictate or v ote on w hich loans ap proved by the IMF   Executive Board can be financed with NAB resources during the activation period.

How does the United States Provide Money to the IMF?

Since 1945, the United States has subscribed about $55 billion as its quota in t he IMF. The Bret   ton Woods A greements A ct prov ides that, u nless Congress agrees by law, the United States cannot provide money or subscri be resources to the IMF. Over the ye   ars, Congress has passed s   everal laws authorizing t he Secretary of the Tre asury to ag ree th at th e Un ited St ates wi ll participate i n IMF fundi ng agreements a nd a uthorizing an d a ppropriating the necessary funds. C ongress has used a variety of budgetary arrange ments to provide this money. A cou ntry's quota in the IMF is a line of cre dit, which is available to the IMF upon r equest when it needs m oney to fund a loan to one of its b orrower co untries. When th e IM F wishes t o draw agai nst the U.S. quota, it asks the New York Federal Reserve Bank to transfer money from the Treasury Depart ment's acc ount t o its ac count so it will h ave th e resourc es necessary for that loan. T he IMF usua lly draws on the resources of severa l countries to fu nd it s lo ans. U.S. fi nancial re lations with the IM F a re o ff-budget. For accounting re asons, payments to the IMF fro m U.S. quota resources have no outlay effect and no impact on the federal budget deficit. As loans are repaid to the IMF, it transfers the borrowed funds back to the United States. T he I MF pay s th e United Sta tes and other c ountries i nterest on the outstanding balance whenever it uses their quota resources.

Table 1. U.S. Banking Exposure to Greece, Ireland, Italy, Portugal, and Spain Amounts Outstanding, Billions of US$, 2010 Quarter 1

Country	Amount
Greece 13.7	
Ireland 73.8	
Italy 51.8	
Portugal 4.9	
Spain 55.3	
Total	**199.5**

Source: B ank f or Intern ational Settlements (BIS), " Consolidated Intern ational Claims of BIS Reporting Banks," provisi onal dat a for 2010 Q1 (m ost r ecent dat a ava ilable), Table 9B: Consolidated Foreign Claims of R eporting B anks - Immediate Borr ower Basis, http://www.bis.org/statistics/consstats.htm.
Notes: Provisional data. Figures may not add exactly due to rounding.

What is the Role of Congress?

Once Congress has approved U.S. participation and provided appropriated funds to back an additional U.S. subscription, it has no further role in the IMF lending process. Neither individual loans nor the IMF's ability to draw against U.S. quota re sources m ust be ap proved i n ad vance by Congress. A t the t ime the United States subscribes to new quota resources, it may not put restrictions on the ways the IMF may use those funds, as th is w ould violate the terms of the I MF funding agre ements. C ongress may enact l egislation r equiring t he U.S. executive director at the IMF to oppose loans to specific countries or for specific p urposes. However, with 16 .8% of the t otal v ote, the Un ited Stat es cannot by itself block approval of loans by the IMF Executive Board.

IMPLICATIONS OF THE EUROZONE DEBT CRISIS FOR THE UNITED STATES

How Strong are the Economic Ties between the United States and the EU?

The United States and the European Union (EU) econ omic relati onship is the l argest in the world— and i t is gro wing.[16] The modern U .S.-European economic relationship has evolved since World War II, broa dening as the si x-member Europe an C ommunity exp anded i nto t he pres ent 27-member European U nion. T he t ies ha ve al so bec ome more co mplex an d interdependent, covering a growing number and type of trade, investment, and financial activities.

In 2009, $1,252.0 billion flowed between the United States and the EU on the current account, the most comprehensive measure of U.S. trade fl ows. The EU as a unit is the largest merchandise trading partner of the United States. In 2009, the EU accounted for $220.6 billion of total U.S. exports (or 20.8%) and for $2 81.8 bi llion of t otal U.S. im ports (or 18 .1%) for a U .S. tra de defi cit of $73.2 b illion. The EU is also t he la rgest U.S. trade partner when trade inservices is added to trad e in merchandise, accounting for $173.5 bi llion (or 34.5% of t he total i n U .S. services e xports) and $1 34.8billion (or 36.4% of total U.S. services imports) in 2009. In addition, in 2009, a net $114.1 billion *flowed* from U.S. residents to EU countries into direct investments, while a net $82.7 bi llion *flowed* fro m EU reside nts to direct i nvestments in th e U nited States.[17]

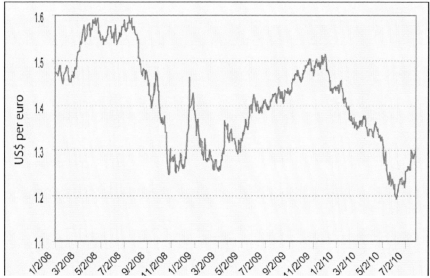

Source: European Central Bank (ECB).

Figure 2. US$/Euro Exchange Rate, January 2008 – June 2010.

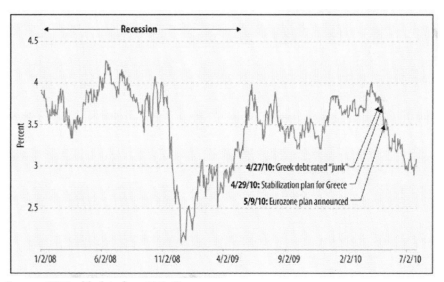

Source: CRS with data from U.S. Treasury.

Figure 3. Yields (Interest Rates) on U.S. 10-year Treasury Notes.

What is the Exposure of U.S. Banks to Vulnerable European Countries?

This table shows only direct bank lending. What is generally not known is the e xposure of U .S. finan cial i nstitutions thro ugh iss uance of cred it defa ult swaps based on Greek sovereign debt. The effect of credit default swaps could be t o l ower U.S. ban k e xposure t o so vereign d ebt b y offsetti ng U.S. ban k liabilities or to raise U.S. bank exposure to sovereign debt if U .S. banks sold credit protection.[18]

How has Financial Instability in the Eurozone Affected the Value of the Dollar?

As investors lost confidence in the future of the Eurozone, and the size of the adjustment require d for the Eurozone as a w hole bec ame appa rent, the value of t he euro bega n t o weaken. The euro de preciated aga inst t he U.S. dollar by 21% between December 12, 2009 and June 8, 2010 (from 1.51$/€ to 1.22$/€; see **Figure 2**). A w eaker euro likely low ers U .S. export s to the Eurozone a nd incre ases U .S. im ports from the Euro zone, w idening the U .S. trade d eficit. On the ot her han d, it m akes purchas es and U .S. inv estments in Eurozone countries cheaper in dollar terms. Beginning in June, the value of the euro rel ative to the U .S. dol lar has b egun to rise b ut has not rea ched its pre-crisis levels (1.30 $/€ on July 27, 2010).

Since the Chinese renminbi has been tied to the value of the dollar, when the dollar appreciates against the e uro, the renminbi also does so . This raises the price of Chinese exports to the Eurozone and lowers the price of European exports to China. This exchange rate e ffect not only affects China's trade with Europe, but it coul d m ake the Unit ed States a m ore attr active market for products from China.

How has the Eurozone Instability Affected U.S. Interest Rates?

Since U.S. Treasury securities are c onsidered to b e a safe have n for investors during times of econo mic turmoil, the immediate effect of the Greek crisis was for inv estors to red uce t heir exposure to euro-deno minated investments, parti cularly those issued by Greece, a nd invest som e of thos e funds in U.S. Treasuries. This caused a greater inflow of funds into the United States and caused the yield on 10-year Treasury notes to fall about one-half of a percentage point (see **Figure 3**). This combined with further pessimism to bring the rate from 4% in April 2010 to about 3% in mid-July. If these lower interest rates persist, U.S. borrowers, including the U.S. Treasury and those seeking mortgages, will benefit. In June 2010, some long-term mortgage interest rates had fallen to as low as 4.25%. For those who rely on interest bearing assets for income, however, lower interest rates reduce the yields they receive on bonds and other securities. In the future, though, if other Eurozone member states default on loans to leveraged banks, global credit markets may shrink by a multiple of the losses as banks deleverage.[19] If this occurs, global interest rates, including those in the United States, could rise.[20]

How Will U.S. Economic Growth be Affected?

The Eurozone instability is affecting the U.S. economy through several economic and financial linkages. The first is in capital flows into the "safe haven" of U.S. Treasury securities and causing lower interest rates as addressed above. The second is in international trade flows. Slower growth in the Eurozone likely will lead to lower U.S. exports there, while the fall in the value of the euro may further reduce the quantity of U.S. exports to the Eurozone but may increase U.S. imports from Europe and travel expenditures there. Slower growth in the Eurozone also is reducing demand for petroleum and lowering the price of oil and other commodities. This will tend to reduce the U.S. import bill for petroleum and tend to increase consumer confidence in the United States. The Eurozone instability, however, also has increased the risk level with respect to sovereign and other debt and has increased volatility in stock markets. While such volatility in the short-term may not affect the overall level of consumption and investment in the United States, a large drop in equity values may reduce consumption through the wealth effect as stockholders see their wealth levels shrink and attempt to save more. Corporations also may find that raising funds for investments through new offerings of stock becomes more difficult.

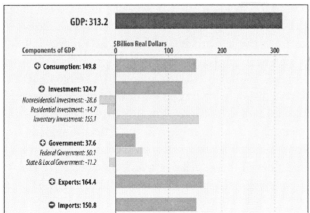

Source: Congressional Research Service with data from U.S. Department of Commerce via IHS Global Insight.

Notes: In billion s of chained 2005 dollars, s easonally adjusted. GDP equals consum ption plus investment plus exports minus imports plus government spending. Subcateg ories for investment (non-residential, residential, a nd inventory) and government spending (federal and state and local) are listed. GDP is estimated various ways and differs from the sum of these components by what is called a residual.

Figure 4. Amount of Change in U.S. Real Gross Domestic Product by Component From First Quarter 2009 to First Quarter 2010.

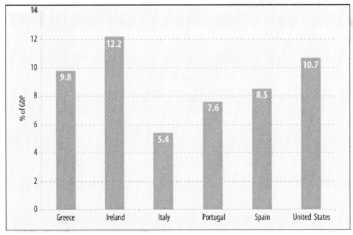

Source: OECD Economic Outlook (No. 87), May 2010.
Notes: Forecasts for general government.

Figure 5. Government Budget Deficits, 2010 Forecasts % of GDP.

Figure 4 shows the amount that real U.S. gross domestic product (GDP) has changed between first quarter 2009 to first quarter 2010. During this time, real GDP increased by $3   13.2 billion. This   consisted of an in crease i n consumption of $149.8 billion, an increase in investment of $1 24.7 billion, an increase i n n et ex ports of $13 .6 b illion, and a n increase i n governm ent expenditures of $37.6 billion.

How will a dr op i n interest rates an d pri ce for petro leum combined with increased risk and a we aker euro affect household c onsumption, th e larg est component in G DP? Th e hig her le vel of risk has   decreas ed c onsumer confidence, but lower interest rates are expected to provide a boost to pent-up demand for consum er durables, the purchase of which tended to be postponed during the rec ession. Consumption is expected to increase in line with GDP. Investment, both by businesses in new plant and equipment and households in residential structures, is a key to U .S. recovery. A s c an be s een in **Figure 4**, the i ncrease i n U.S. investment over t he past year has be en i n i nventory accumulation as busi nesses restoc ked s helves in anticipation of risi ng sa les. Growth i n i nvestments in pl ant a nd equipment an d in h ousing has been negative. Lo wer interes t rates pro vide a posi tive b oost to i nvestments i n general, b ut business expectations of l ess ex port de mand fro m Europ e a nd increased risk of another global slowdown in growth may work to c urtail new investments in production capacity. Also, the first-tim e homebuyer tax credit (part of t he Housing a nd Economic Recov ery A ct o f 200 8, P.L. 110-289) expired in mid-2010, and was expected to have moved some housing demand forward. As f or international trade, the drop i n the value of the e uro and weakened demand in the Eurozone are likely to increase the U.S. tra de deficit beyond that expected as U.S. consumption of imports rises. With the exception of lower interest rates on borrowing, government spending, particularly at t he state a nd local le vel, do es not a ppear t o be si gnificantly affecte d by the Eurozone instability.

The combined effect of these positive and negative forces on U.S. growth is difficult to ascertain, but assuming that the crisis is contained, the net effect arguably will be mildly negative. IHS Global Insight stated that it thinks "the fallout from the Gree k crisis for t he Un ited St ates is likely to be relatively small, mostly in the form of loss of competitiveness for U.S. exporters relative to a euro that should remain weak for the foreseeable future." It expects that the Eurozone crisis "will dent the U.S. recovery, but not derail it" and expects the growth rate of U.S. GDP to fall from 3.7% in first quarter 2010 and 2.4% (preliminary estim ate) in se cond quarter of 2010 to the 2.2% to 2.6% range during the second half of 2010. In June 2010, IHS Global Insight expected the annual growth rate to reach 3.1%, but the preliminary second quarter estimate, a full p ercentage po int be low ex pectations, i ndicates that the e conomy's growth rat e m ay be slow ing t o a bout 2.5% for 2   010 [21] (Th e U.S. GD P contracted by 2.4% i n 2009.) The Ec onomist Intell igence Un it e xpects U.S. growth to be 2.7% in 2010, down from the 3.3 % expected in J une 2010.[22] All of this re duced expectation in growth, however, cannot be at tributed solely to the Eur ozone crisis. Other factors are affecting grow th in t he U nited Stat es (e.g., the winding down of the stimulus package).

How do U.S. Government Budget Deficit and External Debt Levels Compare to those in Vulnerable European Countries?

Some are concerned that Greece's de bt crisis foreshadows t he U nited States' future. It is important to note that the sustainability of a government's debt depends on a   host of differen t fa ctors, s uch a s th e fle xibility of t he exchange rate, the currency in which the government has borrowed, and when the debt is falling due, among others. What may be sustainable for a particular government in a parti cular time may not be true for o ther governments. Some have suggested, for ex ample, that although the U.S. bu dget deficit situation is similar to those in vulnerable European countries, the U.S. fiscal position may be stronger t han these other countries because, for e xample, the Uni ted States has a floating exchange rate, the dollar is an international reserve currency, the U.S. overall l evel of de bt (as a perce ntage of G DP) is low er, an d eco nomic growth is (al beit slowly) returning in the United States.[23] The United States is also considered a safe h aven for inves tments, m aking U.S. bonds attractive on private i nternational ca pital markets and   making it easier for t   he U.S. government to rollover its debt.

LEGISLATIVE DEVELOPMENTS

Enacted Legislation

P.L. 111-203
On May 17, 2010, the Se nate ad opted (94-0) an amendment (S.A mdt. 3986), introduced by Senator John Cornyn, to S. 3217, the Restoring Financial Stability Act of 2010. The Senate passed its version of the fin ancial regulatory

reform bill (H.R. 4173), which included S.Amdt. 3986 on May 20, 2010. The Dodd–Frank Wall Street Reform and Consumer Protection Act (P.L. 111-203) was signed by the President on July 21, 2010.

The original version of t he am endment, ti tled " Restrictions on Use of Federal Funds to Finance Bailouts of Foreign Governments," directed the U.S. Executive Director (USED) at the IMF to : evaluate any IMF loan to a country where the publi c debt exc eeds GDP; determine and certify to Con gress whether t he l oan "will be" repa id; a nd u se t he voice a nd vote of the Uni ted States to oppose any loans where such certification could not be made.

As written, t he im pact of the am endment was unclear. Lar ge IMF packages to advanc ed economies appeared t o be t he Am endment's main concern. H owever, i ts pr ovision w ould ap ply t o al l suc h he avily-indebted countries. Thus, it might require the United States to oppose IMF loans to low-income countries with substantial debts. As of 2009, nine countries had public debt burdens greater than their GDP.[24] Several low income countries are near that level and might exceed it if their GDP levels shrank during the midst of a financial crisis that prompted them to seek IMF aid.

The House-Senate conference on the financial reform bill made changes in the original l anguage of this am endment. Sec tion 1500 of the new law specifies that U.S. representa tives at the IMF must oppose loans to such heavily i ndebted c ountries if it is " not like ly" tha t they will b e repai d. Prospective IMF loans t o l ow-income countri es (th ose elig ible at t he World Bank o nly for lo ans fro m its conc essional a id f acility, t he In ternational Development Association) are exempted from this requirement. Lastly, instead of requ iring a Treasury c ertification, t he new law requires the Treasury Department t o rep ort re gularly t o C ongress ab out c onditions in a ny suc h heavily i ndebted c ountry th at rec eived an IMF loa n d espite U.S. o pposition. These reports would discuss the debt status of the borrower country, economic conditions aff ecting its v ulnerability an d its ab ility to repay , an d i ts de bt management status.

Pending Legislation

FY2011 State, Foreign Operations Bill

The House appears to be considering legislation based on the language of the original Cornyn amendment in the FY2011 State, Foreign Operations Bill. The House S tate-Foreign Operat ions Appropriations Su bcommittee approved a draft FY 2011 bill on June 30, 2010.[25] Congressional Quarterly reports that the draft bill includes an amendment proposed by Representative Granger that would require the Treasury Department to review every IMF loan to countries where t he public debt le vel is greater than 60% the size of t he GDP. If Treasury det ermines that the loa n c annot be rep aid, th e Unite d Sta tes must oppose the loan.[26]

H.R. 5299 and S. 3383

On May 13, 2010, Representative Mike Pence introduced H.R. 5299, a bill titled the "European Bailout Protection Act." Senator Jim DeMint introduced a companion bill, S. 3383, on May 18, 2010. Sec. 2 would require the Secretary of the Treasury to oppose any activation of the expanded New Arrangements to Borrow (NAB) facility that would fund directly or indirectly an IMF loan to a member country of the European Union if it or any other member of the EU has a p ublic debt-to-GDP ratio greater t han 60%. Se c. 3 w ould direct t he Secretary to instruct the USED at the IMF to oppose any assistance directly or indirectly to an EU m ember if any other EU member had a debt-to-GDP ratio above t hat le vel. T he bil ls state i n their hea ding t hat t he pr ovisions are temporary, but no time limitation is provided.

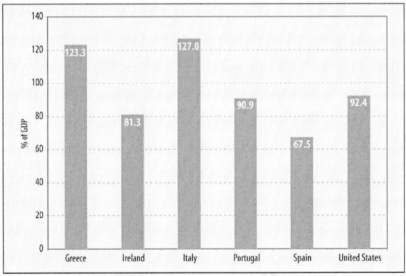

Source: OECD Economic Outlook (No. 87), May 2010.
Notes: Forecasts of general government gross debt.

Figure 6. Public Debt, 2010 Forecasts % of GDP.

Because of t he size of its s hare, the United States can block activation of the expanded NAB facility by withholding support, if and when the expanded NAB co mes i nto effe ct. Th is leg islation would requ ire the Uni ted S tates t o oppose use of the NAB fac ility for any loans to European countries that have substantial p ublic d ebts. So me sugges t, however, t hat th e l egislation m ight also have unintended effects. For example, if this legislation had been in effect last y ear, the United Sta tes would ha ve had t o o ppose all IMF l oans to post-communist co untries of C entral and East ern Euro pe that are m embers of th e EU, even   though m ost analy sts agr ee that e   xcessive le vels of pub   lic indebtedness were not the source of their difficulties.

The bills see m to presum e that the expanded NAB resources wi   ll be activated on   a country-by -country b asis an d t herefore l oans to E   uropean countries can be blocked while loans to other countries may be approved. IMF member countries agreed in April 2010, however, that the expanded NAB will be activated for a set   period of t ime (up to 6 m onths) and w ould be use d t o finance any   applicable loans duri ng t hat period. Th e United St ates has t he power to pre vent the NAB fro m being act ivated but it cannot vet o spec ific borrowers. Under this legislation, the Secretary of the Treasury would need to keep the NAB shut indefinitely or risk the possibility that an EU country might unexpectedly seek   t o   borrow duri ng a   peri od w hen t he N AB   has been activated.

This le gislation m ight also preve nt t he existing b ilateral lin es of c redit provided by so me countries from being folded into the expanded NAB, since this w ould be don e by reim bursing co untries from the N AB for money th e IMF had previously drawn from their bil ateral credits. Bila teral cre dits wer e used to hel p fun d the rec ent loa n to Gree ce. Thus, if this le gislation were in effect, the Unite d States m ight have to oppose act ivation of the NAB for the purpose of reimbursing bilateral creditors for their share in the Greek loan.

Congress has taken no a ction on this le gislation. H owever, the G ranger amendment to t   he p ending fisca l 201   1 Sen ate-Foreign   Operations Appropriations bi ll uses the 6 0% threshold. It might also be i nterpreted as requiring U .S. opp osition t o many proposed IMF lo   ans, th ough t he effect would not be limited solely to loans for European Union countries.

H.Con.Res. 279

On May 18 , 2010, Representative McMorris Ro dgers intr oduced H ouse Concurrent Resol ution 2 79 (H .Con.Res. 27 9), a   measure that w   ould disapprove U.S. partic ipation in a ny IMF funding package for the EU , unl ess each EU m ember country complies with the EU rules on deficit spending a nd each had a public debt-to-GDP ratio at or below 60%. The legislation seeks to discourage or prevent U.S. resources be ing used to he lp fund th e European financial stability pl an announced on May 9, 201 0. T he legislation has be en referred to th e House Com mittee on Fin ancial Servi ces and no furt her acti on has been taken.

ACKNOWLEDGMENTS

Amber Wilhel m, Graphics Specialist, pr ovided assist ance preparing the figures.

End Notes

[1] For the Greek financial assis tance package a nd the broader Eur ozone financial assistance package, the e xchange rate at the time the package was announced is used (approxim ately €1 = $1.31 and €1 = $1.27 respectively). Source: European Central Bank (ECB). However, currency swings are underway, and dollar conversions of data denominated in euros should be approached as estimates.

[2] The loan to Greece was approved by the IMF Executive Board on May 9, 2010.

[3] IMF, "Frequent ly Asked Qu estions: Greece, " May 11, 201 0, htt p://www.imf.org/external/np/exr/faq/greecefaqs.htm.

[4] IMF, "IMF Quotas," March 11, 2010, http://www.imf.org/external/np/exr/facts/quotas.htm.

[5] IMF, "IMF Reaches Staff-level Agreement with Greece on €30 B illion Stand-By Arrangement," p ress release, May 2, 2010 , *http://www.imf.org/external*/np/sec/pr/ 2010/pr10176.htm.

[6] Bob Davis, "IMF's Reach Spreads to Western Europe," *Wall Street Journal*, May 10, 2010.

[7] Ibid.

[8] Andrew Ross Sorkin, "ECB Winds Down Debt Purchases," *New York Times*, July 20, 2010.

[9] Section prepar ed by Marc Labonte, Spe cialist in Macroeconomi c Policy, Government and Finance Division, x7-0640 . For more on the Federal Reserve, see CRS Report RL3 0354, *Monetary Policy and the Federal Reserve: Current Policy and Conditions*, by Marc Labonte.

[10] In response to the beginnings of the recent financial crisis, similar s wap lines were established in December 2007 and expired in February 2010. On the re-establishment of these lines, see Federal Reserve , "Federal Reserv e, Euro pean Cen tral Bank, Ba nk of Canada , Ba nk of England, an d Swiss National Bank Announc e Re establishment of Temporary U.S. Dollar Liquidity Swap Facilities," http://www.feder alreserve.gov/newsevents/press/monetary/20100509a.htm and Federal Reserve, "F OMC Authorizes Re-e stablishment of Temporary U.S. Dollar Liquidity Swap Arrangement wi th the Bank of Japan," http://www.federalreserve.gov/newsevents/press/monetary/20100510a.htm.

[11] CRS Report R40578, *The Global Financial Crisis: Increasing IMF Resources and the Role of Congress*, by Jonathan E. Sanford and Martin A. Weiss.

[12] 148.8 billion IMF Special Dra wing Rights (S DRs). See IMF Financial Activities – Update May 6, 2010 , a vailable at: h ttp://www.imf.org/external/np/tre/activity/2010/071510.htm.

SDR/$ exchan ge rate used is 0   .658957, as of   July 27, 2010   . See *http://www.imf. org/external/np/fin/data/rms_five.aspx* for SDR/$ exchange rates.

[13] The FCC is determined by the IMF's usable resources (including unused amounts under loans and note purchas e agreements), pl us projected loan repayments over the subsequent twelve months, less the   resources that   have al ready been committed u nder existing le nding arrangements, less a prudential balance of 20%   of the quotas of members that   issue the currencies that are used in the financing of IM F transactions to "safeguard the liquidity of creditors' claims and take account of the potentia l erosion of the IMF's resource base." See IMF Financial Activities – Update May 6, 2010, for additional definitions.

[14] IMF Executive Board Approves Major Ex pansion of Fun d's Borrowing Arrangements to Boost Resources for Crisis Resolution, *International Monetary Fund*, April 12, 2010.

[15] To meet the U. S. $ 100 billion commitment to t he expanded NAB, as well as an $8 billion increase in the   U.S. quota at th e IMF, Congress appropriated $5 billion in the FY2009 Spring Supplemental Appropriations for Overseas Contingency Operations (P.L. 111-32).

[16] For more information, see CRS Report RL30608, *EU-U.S. Economic Ties: Framework, Scope, and Magnitude*, by William H. Cooper.

[17] Data from CRS Report RL3   0608, *EU-U.S. Economic Ties: Framework, Scope, and Magnitude*, by William H. Cooper.

[18] For more on credit default swaps, see CRS Report RS22932, *Credit Default Swaps: Frequently Asked Questions*, by Edward V. Murphy and Rena S. Miller.

[19] For example, s ee Frederic S. M ishkin, "On 'Leveraged Losses: Lessons from the Mortgage Meltdown'," Speech at the U.S . Monetary Policy Forum, Ne w York, New York, February 29, 2008, http://www.federalreserve.gov/newsevents/speech/mishkin20080229a.htm.

[20] For more on this point, see CRS Report RL34412, *Containing Financial Crisis*, by Mark Jickling.

[21] IHS Global Insight, U .S. *Executive Summary, Aegean Contagion?*, May 20 10; and U.S . Economy, Eco nomic Commentary: GDP , updated J une 25, 2 010, ac cessed July 28, 2 010. U.S. Burea u of Economic Ana lysis, *National Income and Product Accounts, Gross Domestic Product: Second Quarter 2010 (Advance Estimate)*, BEA Ne ws Release, BEA 10-37, July 30, 2010.

[22] Economist Int elligence U nit, *Forecast for the United States of America*, 2010 , u pdated for August 1, 2010. Accessed July 28, 2010.

[23] E.g., see Paul Krugman, "We're Not Greece," *New York Times*, May 13, 2011.

[24] Greece, Iceland, Italy, Jamaica, Japan, Le banon, Singapore, Suda n and Zimbabwe , according to the Economist Intelligence Unit.

[25] In the absence of a FY2011 budget resolution, both the House and Senate have begun work on FY2011 funding legislation usin g committee- approved discretionary budget allocat ions. The State-Foreign Operations Sub committee was al located $53. 9 billion in the House and $54.0 billion in the Senate.

[26] Joanna Anders on, *Panel Approves Fiscal 2011 State-Foreign Operations Appropriations*, at CQ.com,http://www.cq.com/display.do?dockey/cqonline/prod/data/docs/html/committees/1 11/committees111-2010063000276116.html@committees&metapub=CQ-COMMITTEEMARKUPS&searchIndex=2&seqNum=3.

In: The Eurozone: Testing the Monetary Union   ISBN: 978-1-61209-113-6
Editors: H.J. Farkas and D.C. Murphy   © 2011 Nova Science Publishers, Inc.

Chapter 3

GREECE'S DEBT CRISIS: OVERVIEW, POLICY RESPONSES, AND IMPLICATIONS*

Rebecca M. Nelson, Paul Belkin and Derek E. Mix

SUMMARY

Buildup of Greece's Public Debt: Over the past decade, Greece borrowed heavily in in ternational cap ital markets to fund go vernment bu dget and current account deficits. The profligacy of the government, weak revenue collection, and structural ri gidities in Greece's eco nomy are typ ically cited as m ajor factors behind Greece's accumulation of debt. Access to capital at low interest rates after adopting the euro and weak enforcement of E U rules c oncerning debt and deficit ceilings may also have played a role.

Outbreak of Greece's Debt Crisis: Reliance on financing from international capital markets left Greece   highly vulnera ble to s hifts in investor c onfidence. Investors became j ittery in   October 2009, wh en the n ewly-elected Greek government revised the estimate of the government budget deficit to nearly double the ori ginal number. Over t he ne xt m onths, th e gov ernment an nounced sev eral austerity packages and had successful rounds of bond sales on international capital markets to raise n eeded fun ds. In late April, when E urostat, the Europe an Union

---

* This is an edi ted, reformatted and augmented   version of Cong ressional Research Service publication, Report R41167, dated May 14, 2010.

(EU)'s statistical agency,   further revised the estim ate of Greece's 2009 de ficit upwards, G reek b ond s preads s piked and two m   ajor credit rating agencies downgraded Greek bonds.

Eurozone/IMF Financial Assistance: The Gree k go vernment formally requested financial assistance from the 16 member states of the Eurozone and the International Mo netary Fu nd (IM F), and a   €110 b illion (about $ 145 b illion) package was a nnounced on May 2, 2010. The package a ims to preve nt Greece from defaulting on its de bt obligations and to stem contagion of Greece's crisis to other European countries, including Portugal, Spain, Ireland, and Italy. Despite the substantial size o f th e package, so me e conomists are concerne d that the Eurozone/IMF package m ight not be enough to   prevent Greece from defaulting on, or re structuring, i ts debt, or eve n fr om l eaving t he E urozone. Gree ce's de bt crisis th reatened to wi den acro ss Eu rope, as b ond sp reads for se veral European countries spiked and depreciation of the euro began to accelerate.

On Sund ay, May 9, 2010, EU leaders announced t hat they woul d m ake an additional €500 billion ($6 36 b illion) in fin ancial assistan ce av ailable to vulnerable Europ ean co untries, with th e IMF con tributing up t o an ad ditional €220 b illion (ab out $ 280 b illion) to €250 b illion (about $ 318 b illion). Th e same day, the European Central Bank (ECB) announced it co uld start buying European bonds, a nd t he U.S. Fe deral R eserved al so announced i t wo uld reopen cur rency swap lines   with othe r m ajor central ba nks, in cluding th e ECB, to   help ease economic pressure. W hen mar kets o pened o n Monday, May 10, 2 010, b ond spreads in E urope d ropped a nd t he e uro be gan t o strengthen, s uggesting t hat t he package was successful in stemming the spread of Greece's crisis.

Implications for the United States: Greece's debt crisis could have several implications fo r th e Un ited States. First, fallin   g in vestor con fidence in th e Eurozone has weakened t he eur o, w hich, i n t urn, co uld wi den t he U.S. t rade deficit. Second, given the strong economic ties bet ween the United States and the EU, fi nancial i nstability in the EU cou ld imp act th e U.S. economy. Th ird, $16.6 billion of Greece's d ebt is h eld by U.S. banks, and a Greek d efault wou ld lik ely have ram ifications for the se creditors. Fo urth, some have s uggested that Greece's current debt crisis foresha dows what the United States could face in t he future. Others argue that the an alogy is weak, because the United States, unli ke Greece, has a floating exchange rate and a national currency that is an international reserve currency. Fifth, the debate about im balances within the Euro zone is sim ilar to th e debates a bout U.S. -China imbalances, a nd reiterates ho w, i n a gl obalized economy, the econom   ic polic ies o f one co untry imp act o ther co untries' economies.

INTRODUCTION

Historically, financial crises have been followed by a wave of governments defaulting on their debt obligations.[1] Financial crises tend to lead to, or exacerbate, sharp economic downturns, low government revenues, widening government deficits, and high levels of debt, pushing many governments into default.[2] As recovery from the global financial crisis begins, but the global recession endures, some point to the threat of a second wave of the crisis: sovereign debt crises.[3]

Greece is currently facing such a sovereign debt crisis. On May 2, 2010, the Eurozone members and International Monetary Fund (IMF) endorsed a historic €110 billion (about $145 billion) financial package for Greece in an effort to avoid a Greek default and to stem contagion of Greece's crisis to other European countries, particularly Portugal, Spain, Ireland, and Italy. [4] On May 9, 2010, the European Union (EU) announced an additional €500 billion (about $636 billion) in financial assistance that could be made available to assist vulnerable European countries.

Greece's debt crisis has raised a host of questions about the merits of the euro and the prospects for future European monetary integration, with some calling for more integration and others less. Of heated debate, in particular, is the viability of an economic union that has a common monetary policy but diverse national fiscal policies. Some economists have suggested that Greece could benefit from abandoning the euro and issuing a new national currency, although doing so would raise the real value of Greece's external debt and possibly trigger runs on Greek banks and contagion of the crisis more broadly within the Eurozone.

The United States and the EU have strong economic ties, and a crisis in Greece that threatens to spill over to other Southern European countries could impact U.S. economic relations with the EU and the general economic recovery from the financial crisis. Additionally, the exposure of U.S. banks is estimated at $16.6 billion.[5] The Obama Administration was reportedly supportive of the EU and IMF's decision to offer financial support to Greece and other vulnerable Eurozone economies. Indeed, at least one press report indicates that Administration officials began urging their European counterparts to take decisive action to prevent the possibility of Greek default as early as February.[6] President Obama is reported to have called German Chancellor Angela Merkel and French President Nicolas Sarkozy on May 9, 2010, to encourage them to structure a broader package of financial assistance in an effort to stem possible contagion of the Greek crisis to other Eurozone Members.[7] On May 10, 2010, the U.S. Federal Reserved reopened credit swap lines with the European Central Bank (ECB), among other major central banks, to help ease economic pressures resulting from the crisis in Europe.

Given this context, c ongressional i nterest in Greece's debt c risis is high. Greece's economic situation was a m ajor focus of discussion during Gre ek Prime Minister Geo rge Papa ndreou's m eetings w ith congressi onal lead ers in a v isit t o Washington, DC in March 2010.[8] Numerous congressional hearings in 2010 have referenced Gre ece's econom ic situation, a nd the House Committee on Financial Services h eld a h earing on April 29 , 2010, o n t he i mplications of Greece's debt crisis for credit default swaps. Given the large financial commitment of the United States to the IMF, there is also strong congressional interest in the IMF 's role in providing financial assistance to Greece.

This report provides an overview of the crisis; outlines the major causes of the crisis, focusing on both domestic and i nternational factors; exam ines how Greece, the Eurozone members, and the IMF have responded to the crisis; and highlights the broader implications of Greece's debt crisis, including for the United States.

GREECE'S DEBT CRISIS: BACKGROUND

Buildup to the Current Crisis

During the decade prece ding the global fin ancial crisis th at started i n fall 2008, Greece's governm ent borrowed hea vily from abroad to fund   substantial government bud get an d cu rrent acco unt d eficits.[9] Between 2001, whe n Greece adopted the e uro as its cu rrency, and 2008, Greece 's reported budget deficits averaged 5% per year, com pared to a   Eurozone ave rage of 2%, a nd current account deficits averaged 9% per year, co mpared to a Eurozone ave rage of 1%. [10] In 2009, Greece's budget deficit is estimated to have been more than 13% of GDP. Many at tribute t he b udget a nd current acc ount deficits t o t he high s pending o f successive Greek governments.[11]

Greece funde d these twin   deficits by   borrowing in i nternational c apital markets, leaving it with a chronically high external debt (116% of GDP in 2009).[12] Both Greece's budget   deficit and e xternal debt le vel are   well above those permitted by the rules governing the EU's Economic and Monetary Union (EMU). Specifically, the Treaty on Eu   ropean Union, co mmonly referred to as th e Maastricht Treaty, calls for budget deficit ceilings of 3% of GDP and external debt ceilings of 60% of GDP. Greece is not al one, however, in exceeding these lim its. Of the 27 EU member states, 25 exceed these limits.[13]

Greece's relia nce on external financ   ing for fundi ng budget and curre nt account deficits left its economy highly vulnerable to shifts in investor confidence. Although the outbreak of the g lobal finan cial crisis in fall 2 008 led to a liq uidity crisis for m   any cou ntries, i ncluding se veral C entral and East   ern Eur opean countries, the Greek government initially weathered the crisis relatively well and had been a ble to continue   accessing ne   w funds from international   markets. However, the   global recession resulting fro   m the fina ncial crisis put   strain on many governments' budget s, including   Greece's, as s pending increase d a nd ta x revenues weakened. [14]

Outbreak of the Current Crisis

Since l ate   2009, i nvestor c onfidence i n t he Greek government has   been rattled. In Oct ober 200 9, the n ew so cialist g overnment, led b y Prim e Min ister George Papa ndreou, re vised t he est imate of t he government bu dget deficit f or 2009, nearly doubling the existing estimate of 6.7% of GDP to 12.7% of GDP.[15] This wa s sh ortly fol lowed b y rat ing downgrades of Greek b onds by t he t hree major cred it ratin g ag encies. In late   November 2 009, questions ab out wh ether Dubai World, a st ate-controlled ent erprise i n Dubai, w ould default on i ts de bt raised additional concerns about the possibility of a cascad e of so vereign defaults for go vernments un der th e strain o f th e fin ancial crisis. Co untries with larg e external debts, like   Greece, were of particular c oncern for investors. Allegations that Greek gov ernments h ad falsified statistics an d attem pted to o bscure debt levels through complex financial instruments also contributed to a drop in investor confidence.[16] Before the cri sis, Gree k 10-year bond y ields we re 1 0 t o 40 ba sis points abo ve German 1 0-year bonds. With the crisis, th is spread increased to 400 basis po ints in Janu ary 2010, w hich was at the tim e a record high.[17] High bond spreads indicate declining investor confidence in the Greek economy.

Despite inc reasing nervousness surr ounding Greece's ec onomy, the Greek government was ab le to successfully sell €8 billion ($10.2 billion) in bonds at the end of January 2010, €5 billion ($6.4 billion) at the end of March 2010, and €1.56 billion ($ 1.99 billion) in m id-April 20 10, alb eit at h igh in terest rates. However, Greece m ust borrow an a dditional €54 b illion ($68.8 b illion) to cov er maturing debt a nd i nterest pay ments i n 2010, a nd c oncerns began t o develop a bout t he government's ability to do so.[18]

At t he end o f M arch 20 10, Eur ozone m ember st ates pl edged t o p rovide financial assistance to   Greece in c oncert with t he IM F, if necessary, and if requested by Greece's governm ent. Nego tiations and discussi ons about the package co ntinued an d i nvestor jitteriness sp iked ag ain in April 2 010, wh en Eurostat, the   EU's statistical agency, re leased its estimate of Greece   's budget deficit. At 13.6% of GDP, Eurostat's es timate was alm ost a full pe rcentage point higher tha n the previ ous estimate releas ed by the Gre ek go vernment in October 2009. This led to renewed questions about Greece's ability to repay its debts, with

€8.5 billion ($10.8 billion) falling due on May 19, 2010. On April 23, 2010, the Greek government formally requested financial assistance from the IMF and other Eurozone countries. The European Commission, backed by Germany, requested that more details on Greece's proposed budget cuts for 2010, 2011, and 2012 be released before providing the financial assistance. In late April 2010, the spread between Greek and German 10-year bonds reached a record high of 650 basis points,[19] and one of the major credit rating agencies, Moody's, downgraded Greece's bond rating by one notch. On April 27, 2010, another ratings agency, Standard and Poor's, downgraded Greek bonds to "junk" status.

In meetings with members of the German Parliament (*Bundestag*), IMF Managing Director Dominique Strauss-Kahn reportedly raised the prospect of a three-year assistance package to Greece totaling €120 billion ($152 billion), substantially larger than initially reported in news reports. As negotiations among the IMF, Eurozone member states, and Greece continued, Greece agreed to additional austerity measures. On May 2, 2010, the Eurozone and IMF announced a three-year, €110 billion (about $145 billion) stabilization plan for Greece. Eurozone countries are to contribute €80 billion (about $105 billion) in bilateral loans, pending parliamentary approval in some countries. The IMF is to contribute a €30 billion (about $40 billion) loan at market-based interest rates. The agreement is considered historic, because it is the first IMF loan to a Eurozone country and the overall package is substantial relative to Greece's GDP (forecasted to be €229 billion [$291 billion] in 2010).[20] In exchange for financial assistance, Greece submitted a three-year plan aimed at cutting its budget deficit from 13.6% of GDP in 2009 to below 3% of GDP in 2014. The Eurozone/IMF package was announced amidst Greek protests that at times started turning violent.

Despite the substantial size of the financial assistance package, the threat of Greece's crisis spreading to other Eurozone countries remained. Bond spreads for several other European countries spiked and the euro started to depreciate rapidly. In a bid to "save the euro," on May 9, 2010, European Union governments announced that they would make an additional €500 billion (about $636 billion) available to vulnerable European countries. The IMF may contribute up to an additional €220 billion (about $280 billion) to €250 billion (about $318 billion). Following the announcement, the market reacted positively, as bond spreads for several vulnerable European countries dropped and the euro began to strengthen.

POSSIBLE CAUSES OF GREECE'S CRISIS

Greece's current economic problems have been caused by a mix of domestic and international factors. Domestically, high government spending, structural rigidities, tax ev   asion, and   co rruption h ave all co   ntributed t o Greece's accumulation of debt ove r the past deca de. Internationa lly, the adopti on of the euro and lax enforcement of EU rules ai med at lim iting the accum ulation of de bt are also believed to have contributed to Greece's current crisis.

Domestic Factors

High Government Spending and Weak Government Revenues

Between 2001 and 2007, Gr eece's GDP grew at an ave rage a nnual rate of 4.3%, com pared to a E urozone ave rage of 3.1%.[21] High econ omic g rowth rates were driven primarily by increases in   private co nsumption (l argely f ueled by easier access t o cre dit) and public investm ent financed by the E U and the central government. Over t he past si x y ears, however, w hile cent ral government expenditures i ncreased by 87%, re venues grew by o nly 31 %, l eading t o b udget deficits w ell ab ove th e EU' s agr eed-upon th reshold of 3 %.[22] Obse rvers als o identify a large and inefficient public administration, costly pension and healthcare systems, tax ev asion, and   a g eneral "absen ce of t he will to m aintain fiscal discipline" as major factors behind Greece's deficit.[23]

According t o the OEC D, as of 2004, s pending on public adm inistration as a percentage of total public expenditure in   Greece was hi gher tha n i n a ny ot her OECD member, "with no ev idence that the quantity or quality of the serv ices are superior."[24] Th is tr end h as continued. Greek go vernment ex penditures in 2 009 accounted for 50% of GDP, with 75% of (non-interest) public s pending going t o wages an d soc ial benefi ts.[25] Successi ve G reek g overnments ha ve t aken st eps t o modernize and consolidate the public administration. However, observers continue to cite overstaffing and poor productivity in the public sector as an impediment to improved economic performance. An aging Greek population—the percentage of Greeks aged over 64 is expected to rise from 19% in 2007 to 32% in 2060—could place additional burdens on public spending and what is widely conside red one of Europe's m ost gene rous pe nsion syst ems. Accordi ng to the OECD,   Greece's "replacement rate of 70%-80% of wa ges (plus a ny benefits from suppl ementary schemes) is h igh, and en titlement to a full p ension requ ires only 35 years of contributions, compared t o 4 0 i n m any ot her co untries."[26] Ab sent reform, to tal Greek public pension payments are expec ted to increase from 11.5% of GDP in 2005 to 24% of GDP in 2050.

Weak revenue collection ha s also cont ributed to Greece's budget de ficits. Many econom ists identify tax evasion an d Greece's unrecorded economy as key factors behind the deficits. They argue that Greece m ust address the se problems if it is to raise th e revenues necessary to imp rove its fiscal p osition. Some stu dies have valued the inform al e conomy in Greece at between 25%-30% of GDP. [27] Observers offer a va riety of expl anations for the prevalence of tax e vasion i n Greece, incl uding high level s of ta xation and a c omplex tax c ode, e xcessive regulation, and inefficiency in the public sector. Like his pre decessor Constantine (Costas) Karamanlis, Prime Minister Papandreou has committed to cracking down on tax and s ocial security contribution e vasion. Observers note, however, that past Greek gove rnments have had, at best , mixed success seeing through sim ilar initiatives.

Structural Policies and Declining International Competitiveness

Greek in dustry is su ffering fro m d eclining in ternational co mpetitiveness. Economists cit e h igh relativ e wag es an d low produ ctivity as a p rimary facto r. According to one st udy, wages in Greece have increased at a 5% annual rate since the country adopte d the euro, about double the average rate in the Eurozone as a whole. Over the same period, Greek exports to its major trading partners grew at 3.8% per y ear, o nly hal f t he rate o f t hose countries' imports f rom ot her t rading partners.[28] Some obse rvers argue that for Greece to boost the c ompetitiveness of its i ndustries and re duce i ts curre nt acc ount defi cit, i t needs t o i ncrease i ts productivity, s ignificantly cu t wage s, a nd i ncrease sa vings. A s discussed below, the Papandreou government has begun t o curb public sect or wages a nd hopes t o increase Gree k exports through investm ent in areas where the country has a comparative advantage. In the past, t ourism and t he s hipping industry have been the Greek economy's strongest sectors.

International Factors

Increased Access to Capital at Low Interest Rates

Greece's adoption of the euro as its national currency in 2001 is seen by some as a contri buting fact or in Greece's buildup of debt. W ith the c urrency bloc anchored by econom ic h eavyweights Ge rmany and France , and a comm on monetary pol icy conse rvatively managed by t he EC B, i nvestors ha ve tended t o view th e reliab ility o f eu ro member co untries with a h eightened deg ree of confidence. Th e p erceptions o f stab ility conferred b y eu ro m embership allo wed Greece, as well as other Eurozone members, to borrow at a more favorable interest rate th an would lik ely hav e been th e case ou tside t he EU, m aking it easier to finance the state budget and service existing debt. This benefit, however, may also have contributed to Greece's current debt problems: observers argue that access to artificially cheap credit allowed Greece to a ccumulate high levels of de bt. Critics assert t hat i f the market had di scouraged excess bo rrowing by making debt financing more expensive, Greece would have been forced to come to terms earlier with the need for austerity and reform.

Issues with EU Rules Enforcement

The lack of en forcement o f th e Stab ility and Growth Pact is a lso seen as a contributing factor t o Greece's high level of debt. In 1997, EU m embers adopted the Stab ility an d Gro wth Pact, an agreemen t to enhance th e su rveillance and enforcement of the public fin ance rules set o ut in th e 1992 Maastricht Treaty's "convergence criteria" for EMU. The rules call for government budget deficits not to excee d 3% of GDP and public de bt not to exceed 60% of GDP. The 1997 Stability and Growth Pact cl arified and sped up the ex cessive deficit procedure to be applied to member states that surpassed the deficit limit. If the member state is deemed to have in sufficiently co mplied with th e co rrective measures recommended by t he Eur opean C ommission an d t he C ouncil of t he E uropean Union during the excessive deficit procedure, the process may ultimately result in a fine of as much as 0.5% of GDP.[29]

Following the l aunch of the euro in 1 999, an increasing num ber of member states found it h ard to comply with th e limits set b y the Pact. Sin ce 2003, m ore than 30 e xcessive de ficit pr ocedures h ave bee n undertaken, with t he EU reprimanding member states and pressuring them to consolidate public finances, or at least promise to do so. The EU, however, has never imposed a financial sanction against any member state for violating the deficit limit. The lack of enforcement of the Stability and Growth Pact is th ought to have limited the role the EU can play in discouraging countries, like Greece, from running up high levels of debt.

The Europ ean Co mmission initiated an excessiv e deficit pro cedure again st Greece in 2004 whe n Greec e reported an upward re vision of its 2003 budget deficit fi gure to 3. 2% of GDP. I n its rep ort, the C ommission i ndicated t hat "t he quality o f public d ata is n ot satisfacto ry," noting th at th e EU's statistical o ffice, Eurostat, had not ce rtified or had u nilaterally am ended dat a p rovided by t he National Statistical Service of Greece since 2000.[30] Subsequent statistical revisions between 2 004 an d 2007 revealed that Greece ha d violated the 3% lim it in e very year si nce 2 000, wi th i ts d eficit t opping out at 7. 9% of GDP i n 2004. T he Commission also note d that Greece's de bt had been above 100% of GDP since before Greece joined the euro, and that the statistical revisions had pushed the debt number up as well. The E U cl osed the excessive de ficit procedure in 2 007, with the Co mmission pronouncing itself satisf ied th at G reece h ad tak en su fficient measures, "mainly of a permanent nature," and that the country's deficit would be 2.6% of GDP in 2006 and 2.4% in 2007.

The Co mmission also conclu ded th at "th e Greek st atistical au thorities improved t heir p rocedures," l eading to "an overall h igher quality o f data."[31] The Commission opene d a new excessive deficit proce dure i n 2009 when Greece's

2007 deficit was reported at 3.5% of GDP, and that procedure is ongoing in the context of the current situation.[32] This points to a broader problem of a monetary union without a fiscal union, as discussed below in "European Integration."

ADDRESSING GREECE'S CRISIS: PROGRESS TO DATE

The Greek government faces government budget and current account deficits that it can no longer finance by borrowing from international capital markets. Some caution that Greece is at risk of defaulting on its debt obligations. To address this crisis, the government is pursuing a mix of fiscal austerity (government spending cuts and tax increases) and structural reforms to improve the competitiveness of the economy. Financial assistance from the other Eurozone member states and the IMF is allowing the adjustment to take place over a longer time period. Some economists have concern that despite the government's reforms and the financial assistance from other Eurozone member states and the IMF, the Greek government may still default on or restructure its debt and/or leave the Eurozone. Amidst concerns that Greece's crisis spreading throughout the Eurozone, the EU has announced it will make substantial resources available to vulnerable European countries.

Greek Domestic Policy Responses

Fiscal Austerity

Since taking office in October 2009, the Papandreou government has unveiled four separate packages of fiscal austerity measures aimed at bringing Greece's government deficit down from an estimated 13.6% of GDP in 2009 to below 3% by 2014.[33] The government had hoped that three rounds of spending cuts and tax increases announced between January 2010 and March 2010 would restore enough investor confidence in the Greek economy to eliminate the need for outside financial assistance. Financial markets did not react as hoped, and in late April 2010, the Greek government requested assistance from the IMF and EU. The IMF and EU, in turn, called on Athens to implement additional austerity measures. In an emotional and contentious vote, the Greek parliament approved the latest measures on May 6, 2010.

The Papandreou government's three-year fiscal consolidation plan is centered on deep cuts to public spending and enhanced revenue growth through tax increases and a crack-down on tax and social security contribution evasion. On the spending side, most of the cuts focus on the civil service. They include a reduction or freeze on a ll civil service pe nsions, wages, and bonuses and a civi l servant hiring freeze in 2010 with a 5:1 retirement/recruitment ratio for new public sector hires from 20 11. O n t he re venue si de, t he g overnment has raised t he avera ge value-added t ax rat e from 19% t o 23% a nd i ncreased t axes on fuel, tobacco, liquor, and luxury products, among other things.[34] The government hopes to raise revenues e quivalent t o 1.8% o f GDP t hrough st rengthened t ax col lection a nd higher contribution requirements for tax evaders.

Eurozone member states have welcomed the Papandreou government's plans for fiscal consolidation. Some observers express concern, however, that the mix of tax i ncreases and sharp spe nding c uts c ould l ead t o higher unemployment and deepen an ongoing recessi on i n t he count ry. The pol icy sol utions t o t wo of t he major econom ic issues facing the Greek government— cutting large government budget defi cits (whi ch re quires cont ractionary fi scal po licies t o addr ess) an d stimulating the econom y duri ng cyclical eco nomic d ownturn (w hich r equires expansionary fiscal policies) —are at odds with each ot her. Som e question, then, how l ong th e g overnment will b e ab le to coun t on public supp ort for the contractionary measures in the face of a sharp recession.[35]

Structural Reforms

Prime Minister Papa ndreou has re peatedly em phasized t he nee d f or l onger-term structural reforms to the Greek economy. To this end, he has proposed wide-ranging re forms t o t he pen sion a nd health care systems and to Greece's public administration. Hi s government has al so announced m easures t o boost Gree k economic co mpetitiveness by enh ancing e mployment an d economic g rowth, fostering increased private sector development, and sup porting research, technology, and innovation.

As m entioned above, the Gre ek pension sy stem, consi dered o ne o f the most generous i n E urope, has l ong been a t arget of ad vocates of Gree k economic reform. The Papandreou g overnment has pl edged both t o reform pe nsion institutions and to crack do wn on so cial secu rity co ntribution ev asion. Th e government h as said it will raise th e av erage retirem ent ag e fro m 6 1 t o 63 (the statutory retirement age in Greece is 65) a nd be gin calculating pe nsions on the basis of lifetime contributions as opposed to the last five y ears of earnings, as is now th e case with so me civil serv ice p ension sch emes.[36] Prim e Minister Papandreou has an nounced a sim ilar effort t o t ighten pu blic re gulation a nd strengthen accountability in what is widely considered an in efficient Greek health care syste m. His gove rnment also h opes to restructure Greec e's public administration. Th is in cludes co nsolidating l ocal governa nce struct ures by reducing the lev els of local administrative authorities from fiv e to three, reducing the n umber of Greek m unicipalities fro m 1,034 to 370 , and redu cing th e leg al public entities formed by local authorities from 6,000 to 2,000.

Challenges and Prospects

Some economists express   conce rn that Greece's   relatively   drastic contractionary fi scal pol icies coul d pr olong an o ngoing re cession i n the country. GDP contracted by 2% in 2009 and is forecasted to contract by anywhere from 3% to 5% in 2010 and by 0.5% to 1.6% in 2011.[37] Registered unemployment reached 10.6% in Nove mber 2009, the highest level since Ma rch 2005, and is expected to increase in 2010 and 2011. As of October 2009, 27.5% of young people (aged 15-24) in Greece were unemployed. [38]

The Papandreou government hopes to counter these trends by attracting new foreign investment in Greece and by boosting e xports of g oods and se rvices. In addition to adv ancing in stitutional refo rms d esigned to mo re efficien tly d isburse Greek an d E U i nvestment and development fu nds, i t i ntends t o t arget sect ors where it believes Greece has strong co   mparative advantag es for trade and investment. These in clude its g eographic location, particularly as a p otential hub for re gional t rade a nd i nvestment i n ene rgy an d t ransportation networks; t he renewable ene rgy sect or; and al ready st rong gl obal shipping and tourism sectors. Most agree, however, that the challenges to building sustainable economic growth are conside rable. Gree k exports droppe d by clo se to 18 % in 200 9, an d Greek businesses have become increasingly uncompetitive in domestic and international markets.[39]

Perhaps t he m ost s ubstantial chal lenge f or t he G reek government coul d be maintaining public and   political su pport fo r its au sterity an d eco nomic refo rm program. Papandreou's Panhellenic Socialist Movement (PASOK) came to office in Oct ober 2009 o n a platform of "soci al protection" p romising t o b oost wa ges, improve support for the poor, and promote redistribution of income. The policies his government has since pursued to cut the budget deficit have required retreating from most of t hese cam paign pl edges and could prove pol itically difficult to see through. Thousands of public sector workers and their supporters have taken to the streets to   protest the a usterity measures a nd m ore protests are   scheduled. T he protests turn ed d eadly on May 5 , 201 0, when three people were killed during an attack on an At hens ban k. Despi te gr owing p ublic op position to hi s austerity program, Papan dreou h as secu red parliamentary suppo rt of th e m easures. A majority of Greeks appear to recognize th e need for fi scal cons olidation and se e PASOK as t he m ost cred ible p olitical p arty to see t his th rough. Ob servers emphasize, however, that support for Papandreou could be contingent on whether his gove rnment's austerity measure s are se en as fair an d just. In th is reg ard, th e focus on re forming w hat is widely vi ewed as a co rrupt and bloated public sect or could benefit Papandreou.

Greece's large st opposition   party, th e ce nter-right New Dem ocracy (ND) unseated by PASOK in the   2009 elections , sup ported the first th ree ro unds of fiscal con solidation m easures t aken by the Papandreou government, but opposed the May 6, 2010, m easures. ND criticized Papandreou's decision to call fo r IMF assistance, with ND party leader Antonis Sam aras predicting th at the "IMF is going to force new measures upon [Greece] that neither [the Greek] economy nor [Greek] so ciety will b e ab le to b ear."[40] Long-tim e observers of Greece point out that th e r eform r ecord of past G reek gover nments d ating b ack t o th e 1 980s is mixed at best. It rem ains t o be seen whether t he Papandreou g overnment wi ll maintain th e public sup port and political will to see thro ugh its wide ran ge of reform proposals.

Eurozone/IMF Financial Assistance to Greece

On May 2, 2010, Eurozone finance ministers and the IMF agreed on a three-year program of loans to Greece totaling €110 billion (about $145 billion): €80 billion (about $105 billion) from Eurozone member states and €30 billion (about $40 billion) fro m th e IMF. The package could repo rtedly p rovide €30 b illion (about $40 billion) from the Eurozone and €10 billion (about $13 billion) from the IMF in 2010 to help e nsure that Greece meets its immediate payment obligations.[41] The brea kdown of the financial assistance pac kage for Greece i s shown in **Figure 1** and discussed in greater detail below.

Eurozone Member States

Details on Eurozone Member State Assistance to Greece
Over th e cou rse o f Mar ch an d April 2 010, Eu rozone lead ers in crementally formulated a mechanism for providi ng financial assista nce to Greec e. Afte r considerable negotiation, lead ers ag reed that t he Eur ozone c ountries wo uld provide bilateral loans, at a market-based interest rate (approximately 5%, which is lower tha n what Greece ha d pai d in recent bond sale s), if s upplemented by additional lo ans fro m th e IMF and if th e Greek government i mplemented substantial au sterity measures o ver th e next th ree year s. On April 23, 2010, th e Greek go vernment fo rmally req uested th e activ ation o f this mechanism an d th e final package was announced the following week.

Of the Eurozone m ember states, Germany i s reportedly providing the largest loan, expected to be €22.4 billion (about $29 billion) over the three-year period, followed by France, wh ich is expected t o loan Greece €16.8 b illion (ab out $22 billion).[42] With payment deadlines on Greek bonds looming, European leaders are aiming t o e xecute t he l oan ar rangements qui ckly. D ue t o di fferent l egal requirements am ong Eurozone countries—final ap proval r equires a pa rliamentary vote in some countries—the loans will likely not all be available at the same time.

Advocates of qui ck implementation o vercame a major hur dle, how ever, when the German parliament approved German participation in the plan on May 7, 2010.

Debates over Eurozone Member State Involvement

Prior to the   decision to loan Greece money, t   he debate about potential Eurozone as sistance was c ontentious. So me observers argued t hat there are compelling reasons for the other Eurozone countries to intervene, asserting that the financial stability of the Eurozone, and possibly even the future of the euro, might be at stak e. Sev ere i nstability in th e Greek economy h ad already started to h ave wider consequences—the crisis contributed to a weake ning of the euro a nd raised concerns that it could spread across European bond markets and draw in countries such as Spain, Portugal, Italy, and Ireland.

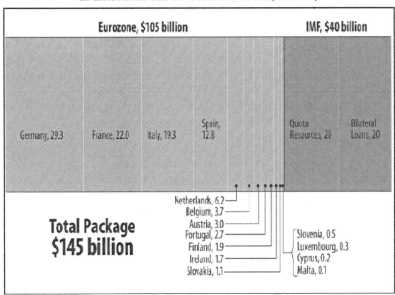

Source: Graphic prepared b y CRS using da ta from Jan Strupczewski, "Factbox - Progress Towards Approving Emergen cy Loans to Greece," *Reuters*, May 6, 2010. IMF data from IM F, "Frequently A sked Ques tions: Greece ," May 11, 20   10, http://www.imf.org/external/np/exr/faq/greecefaqs.htm#q23.

Notes: Eurozone member state commitments are bilateral loans, and some commitments are subject to par liamentary appro val. IMF quota resources and bilateral loans fund a Stand-By Arrangement (SBA) loan for Greece. Conversion to dollars from euros using exchange rate of €1 = $1.318.

Figure 1. Eurozone/IMF Financial Assistance Package for Greece.

Some o bservers no te th at the G reek cr isis grew worse as E urozone le aders contemplated a resp onse—critics ch arge that q uicker acti on m ay h ave ste mmed the crisis at an earlier stag e. There is also a sign ificant political ele ment to t he debate. Monetary union is seen by many proponents of a strong EU as a crowning achievement of Eu ropean i ntegration. S ome obse rvers, t herefore, assert t hat t he EU m ust maintain so lidarity an d t hat th e co untries of th e Eu rozone cann ot not allow Greece to default, much less abandon the euro.

At the sam e tim e, there was also great re luctance to provi de assistance to Greece. Many Euroz one countries are themselves experie ncing financial difficulties, and m any are ex asperated b y th e id ea of rescu ing a cou ntry th at, in their perspective, has not exercised budget di scipline, has fai led to m odernize its economy, an d h as allegedly falsified p ast fin ancial statistics. In ad dition, m any strongly wi sh to av oid setting a prece dent by "bai ling out" a cou ntry that has n ot managed its finances well. Some observers argued that allowing Greece to default could be preferable t o a E urozone rescue packa ge, a nd som e have advocated devising a mechanism to remove countries from the Eurozone that do not meet the requirements. Others have argu ed th at th e Euro zone l oans are illeg al under EU treaties or national laws. German y, the Eurozone's largest economy and arguably its most influential n ational v oice on economic p olicy, has b een am ong the most skeptical member states. Polls show th at a l arge majority of Germans are strongly against provi ding fina ncial assistance to Greece, and Ge rman Chancellor Angel a Merkel repeatedly put a brake on discussions about formulating a rescue package before ultimately assenting.

IMF

Details on IMF Assistance to Greece

Approximately one-third of t he Eurozone and IM F fi nancial package for Greece is from IMF resource s. The IMF assistance to Greece is a three-year, $40 billion lo an mad e at m arket-based in terest rates. Sp ecifically, it is a th ree-year Stand-By Ar rangement (SB A), which i s the IM F's st andard l oan vehicle fo r addressing balance-of-payments d ifficulties. Th e IMF does n ot d isburse th e fu ll amount of its loans to governments at once . Instead, the IMF will divi de the loa n into tranc hes (Fre nch for "sl ice") and w ill only disburse the next tranche afte r verifying that the specified economic policy reforms have been met. Urging policy reforms in this way ensures t hat the loans will b e repaid to the IMF,[43] and that the required economic reforms are implemented.

Greece's loa n from the Fund is unus ual for two reas ons. First, the IMF doe s not ge nerally lend t o de veloped co untries and ha s ne ver l ent t o a Eur ozone member state since the euro was introduced in 1999 as an accounting currency and

2002 as physi cal curre ncy in circu lation. Second, it is unusual for its relative magnitude. The IMF has ge neral lim its on the am ount it will lend to a country either through a SBA o r Extended Fund Facility (EFF), which is similar to a SBA but f or c ountries faci ng l onger-term bal ance-of-payments pr oblems. The IM F's guidelines for l imits on t he si ze of l oans fo r SB As a nd EF Fs are 2 00% o f a member's quota annually and   600% of a me mber's quota cumulatively.[44] IM F quotas are t he fina ncial commitment that IMF members mak e u pon jo ining th e Fund a nd are br oadly ba sed o n t he IMF member's rel ative si ze i n t he w orld economy. In "exceptional" situations, the IMF reserves the righ t to lend in excess of these limits, and has done so in the pa st. The IMF 's loan to Greece i s indeed exceptional ac cess at 3,200% of Greece's IMF quota and is the largest access of IMF quota resources granted to an IMF member country.[45]

The IMF is expected to finance half of Greece's loan ($20 billion) using IMF quota r esources. A lthough the U nited States h as con tributed 17 % of I MF qu ota resources, it is unclear what portion of the IMF loan for Greece that is financed by quota resou rces will b e fu nded b y th e U.S. qu otas. Th e IMF do es not d isclose country contributions to individual transactions with the Fund. In deciding which quota resou rces to u se, t he IMF aim s to p rovide a b alanced position for all members.

The o ther h alf ($ 20 b illion) of th e IMF loan is ex pected to be fin anced b y bilateral loans that have been committed to the IMF as p art of an overall effort to increase IMF resources. None of t his portion is coming from the United States. In 2009, the United States d id agree to ex tend a lin e of cred it worth $100 billion as part o f expanding the IM F's New Arrangements to Borr ow (NAB). However, the expanded NAB is no t yet op erational, so this $100 b illion lin e of cred it from the United States cannot be tapped for Greece's package.

Debates over IMF Involvement

At th e onset of th e Greek crisis, m any EU officials we re insistent that the Eurozone take ownership of the issue. Analysts asserted that it was im portant for the Eurozone to demonstrate its strength and cred ibility by tak ing care of its o wn problems. The pro spect o f "out side" i ntervention from the IMF was viewed by many as a po tential "h umiliation" for th e Eurozone, with officials at th e ECB , among others, str ongly op posed.[46] In late March , however, t he deb ate in Eu rope appeared to shift, with the door slowly opening for possible IMF involvement as a number of me mber states ca me to fa vor a twin -track app roach co mbining Eurozone and IMF financial assistance.

In th e end , IMF in volvement was reportedly a k ey co ndition of Ger man Chancellor Merk el's willin gness to prov ide financial assistan ce to Greece. So me argue that the policy reforms (conditionality) attached to an IMF loan would lend additional im petus to reform and provide both the Greek government and the EU with an outside scapegoat for pushing through politically unpopular reforms. The EU would also make policy reforms a condition of loans, but the IMF is seen as more independent than the EU and has more experience in resolving debt crises than the EU.[47]

Are the Domestic Reforms and Eurozone/IMF Package for Greece Enough?

Some economists fear that Greece's fiscal austerity plan, which entails cutting budget deficits by 9 % o f GDP in fo ur years, is too ambitious an d will be politically difficult to implement.[48] As a result, some economists suggest that the Greek government could still default on or, considered more plausible, restructure its debt. In fact, some observers regret that debt restructuring was not included in the IMF package in order to provide a more orderly debt workout.[49] Restructuring would also push some of co sts of t he crisis onto private banks that, it is argued, engaged i n " reckless l ending" t o Greece.[50] H owever, a default or de bt restructuring could accelera te the contagi on of the c risis to othe r Eurozone countries, as well as hinder Greece's a bility to regain access to capital markets. In addition, eve n if Greece's government stopped servicing its de bt, it would still need s ubstantial fiscal aust erity measures to add ress the gov ernment d eficit unrelated to debt payments.

This has led some economists to argue that Greek fiscal austerity should be offset by m ore accommodating monetary policy by the E CB. This seems unlikely in l ight o f recent re ported c omments by t he Presid ent of th e ECB, Jean -Claude Trichet, on the ECB's commitment to price stability.[51]

As a result, some economists have suggested that Greece should or may leave the Eurozone.[52] This would likely require abandoning the euro, issuing a n ational currency, and allowing that currency t o depreciate a gainst the euro. T he Gree k government would also probably ha ve to put restrictions on bank withdrawals to prevent a run on t he banks du ring th e tran sition fro m th e eu ro t o a n ational currency. It is th ought th at a n ew national currency de preciated against the euro would spur e xport-led growt h in Greece a nd offset t he c ontractionary effects of austerity. Sinc e Greece's debt is denom inated in euros, howeve r, leaving the Eurozone i n f avor of a depreciated nat ional curre ncy w ould rai se t he val ue of Greece's debt in terms of nat ional currency and put pressure on other vulnerable European coun tries. Additionally, so me arg ue th at a Greek departure from th e Eurozone would be ec onomically cat astrophic, creat ing t he "m other of al l financial crises,"[53] and have serious ramifications for political relations among the European states and future European integration.

Broader EU Stabilization Package

EU Member States

Despite the enactm ent of the Euroz one-IMF assistance package for Greece, investor con cerns abo ut t he sustainability of Euro zone deb t d eepened during the first week of May 2010. Driven down by such fears, global stock markets plunged sharply on May 6 , 2010, and th e eu ro fell to a 15-month low ag ainst the do llar. Seeking to head off the possibility of contagion to countries such as Portugal and Spain, EU finance ministers agreed to a broader €500 billion (about $686 billion) "European Financial Stabilization Mec hanism" o n May 9 , 2010. So me an alysts assert that such a bold, large-scale move had become an urgent imperative for the EU i n order t o break t he m omentum of a gat hering E uropean financial cri sis. Investors react ed positivel y to the announce ment of the new agreem ent, with global sto ck markets rebounding on May 10, 20 10, to re-gain the sharp losses of the week before.

The bulk of the European Financial Stabilization Mechanism package consists of a " Special Pu rpose Vehicle" un der which E urozone cou ntries c ould m ake available b ilateral lo ans and g overnment-backed l oan guaran tees t otaling up to €440 billion (about $560 billion) to stabilize the euro area. The agreement, which expires a fter t hree y ears, re quires parliamentary rat ification i n s ome Eur ozone countries. The mechanism a dditionally all ows th e European Co mmission to raise money on ca pital markets and l oan up t o €60 b illion (about $ 76 billio n) to Eurozone st ates. P reviously, suc h a procedure c ould only be ap plied t o non-Eurozone m embers of t he EU, an d was used aft er t he global fi nancial cri sis t o improve the balance-of-pay ments situati ons of Latv ia, Hungary, an d Ro mania. Lastly, the ECB may take on a more significant new role: if necessary to increase market confi dence, t he EC B can now buy member state bonds, a n activity in which it has not previously engaged.

IMF

The Eu ropean Fin ancial Stab ilization Mech anism was an nounced with th e IMF con tributing up to an ad ditional €220 b illion to €250 billion (abo ut $28 0 billion to $318 b illion). This is in lin e with the Greece package, wh ere the Eurozone states contributed roughly 2/3 and the IMF 1/3. IMF Managing Director John Lipsky reportedly later clarified the news reports about the IMF contribution to the European Financial Stabilization Mechanism, saying that these pledges were "illustrative" of th e support th at th e IMF cou ld prov ide.[54] Repo rtedly, Lip sky reiterated t hat the IMF only provides l oans to c ountries that have re quested IMF assistance and that Greece is the only Eurozone country to date that has requested IMF assistance.

IMPLICATIONS OF GREECE'S CRISIS

Contagion and Eurozone Debt Concerns

Prior to th e agreem ent o n the Europ ean Fi nancial Stab ilization Mech anism, growing sp reads on Por tuguese an d Sp anish bo nds, coup led w ith th e late A pril 2010 downgrades of those countries' credit ratings, raised renewed concerns about the po ssibility of co ntagion within t he Euro zone. Con cerns abo ut a sp illover of Greece's crisis to its neighbors are rooted in memories of the Asian financial crisis in 1997-1998, where it is believed that investor herding behavior contributed to the spread of the crisis throughout the region.[55]

As in vestors beco me increasingly n ervous about th e su stainability o f so me countries' debt, the higher interest rates demanded for new bonds make it in turn more d ifficult fo r tho se co untries to bo rrow and to service th eir ex isting debt. Should a l oss of market confidence take hold and spread, investors could rush to sell off the bonds they hold and decline to buy new bonds that countries seek to auction: a cascade of sovereign debt crises could result. While investor confidence is based primarily on conditions within each country, confidence in this case h ad also been affected by the gradual reaction to the Greek crisis, as s ome observers came to doubt the willingnes s and ability of the Euroz one and the IMF to tackl e another crisis in Europe.

The European Financial Stabilization Mechanism appears to have successfully reassured t he m arkets and diminished t he l ikelihood o f a Euroz one cont agion scenario for the time being. Ne vertheless, s ome obs ervers as sert that the mechanism does not s olve the root ca uses o f t he p roblem, and t hat numerous European countries will still need to take difficult steps to increase their industrial competitiveness and improve the state of their public finances. Portugal and Spain had been thought by many to be the leading candidates for the next potential crisis, and Italy and Ireland have been f requently mentioned as wel l. Al though t hese countries all borrowe d hea vily duri ng t he credit bubble t hat precede d t he gl obal financial crisis, the ec onomic circumstances and challenges d iffer in each one. In noting the size of the Italian and Spanish economies compared to the much smaller Greek, I rish, and P ortuguese econ omies, obser vers caut ion t hat a fi nancial cri sis affecting o ne of t he l arger countries c ould p ose a problem of a much hi gher magnitude.

Complex Financial Instruments and Financial Regulation

Through the crisis, it h as been reported that Greek governments, underwritten by pro minent fin ancial in stitutions in cluding Go ldman Sach s, u sed co mplex financial instruments to conceal the true level of Greece's debt.[56] For example, the government of Papa ndreou's predeces sor, Costas Karamanlis, is allege d to ha ve exchanged future revenues from Greece's highways, airports, and lotteries for up-front cas h payments from i nvestors. Li kewise, i t i s r eported t hat t he G reek government bo rrowed b illions b y trad ing currencies at fav orable ex change rates. Because these transactions were technically considered currency swaps, not loans, they did not need to be reported by the Greek government under EU accounting rules. The Federal Reserv e is cu rrently investigating the role th at Goldman Sachs and other U.S. financial institutions played in the buildup of Greece's debt.[57]

The role of complex financial instruments in Greece's debt crisis has exposed some t ensions bet ween t he United States and t he EU over financial regul ation. Some Eu ropean lead ers have called fo r tigh ter financial regu lation, in cluding a prohibition on d erivatives that are believed to have helped create Greece's debt crisis. Financial regul atory r eform before Congress w ould re gulate, but not ban, derivatives. I n a mid-March 20 10 vi sit t o Washington, DC , Pri me Minister Papandreou vocally criticiz ed "unp rincipled sp eculators" for "m aking b illions every day by betting on a Greek default."[58]

European Integration

Greece's debt crisis has also launched a number of broa der debates about the EU's m onetary uni on. Since the introduction of the euro in 1 999, skeptics have pointed to a m ismatch between the EU's advanced economic and monetary union and an incomplete political union. Ev en within the economic areas wh ere the EU is more tig htly in tegrated, th e Eu rozone has a sing le monetary p olicy b ut 16 separate (if l oosely co ordinated) n ational fiscal p olicies. Critics arg ue t hat th is arrangement is p rone to problems an d i mbalances th at t hreaten th e v iability o f having a c ommon currency. Others assert that the Greek crisis points to the need for stronger EU economic governance, at the very least in the form of a tighter and more en forceable Stab ility an d Growth Pact. Go ing furth er, so me p roponents of deeper integration would like to use the crisis to launch a discussion about moving towards a more integrated EU-wide fiscal policy.

Additionally, some officials and analysts have proposed that the E U create a new Eu ropean M onetary F und (EM F) t hat wo uld al low i t t o respond m ore smoothly to fin ancial crises with in ind ividual m ember states in th e fu ture, operating much like the IMF but on a regional, rather than global, basis. There is some discussion that this would require a new governing treaty for the EU, which may be politically difficult to pass. Following the Asian financial crisis in 1997-1998, sim ilar proposals for creating an institution lik e t he IMF, bu t operating specifically within the region, were discussed but no such institution was created. Finally, Greece's crisis has brought to light imbalances within the Eurozone. Some Northern Eu ropean c ountries, suc h as Germany, ha ve rel ied on e xports f or economic gro wth a nd pursued policies that aim t o pr omote such e xport-led growth, such as wage m oderation to keep the costs of production l ow and make exports competitive. Combined with conservative fiscal policies that promote high levels of sa vings, these c ountries ha ve run large c urrent acco unt surpluses. In contrast, s ome Southern E uropean c ountries, like Greece, have had higher levels of wage growth and more expansionary fiscal policies, leading to less com petitive exports an d l ower l evels of savi ngs. T hese co untries have run l arge cur rent account deficits and borrowed to finance these deficits.

Some argue t hat t he Sout hern Eu ropean count ries now need to re duce their debt and increase savings, which translates to running current account surpluses.[59] Hopes for export-led growth may be difficult to realize, however, in the face of the global economic recession. Greece's reliance on tourism, which is highly affected by economic conditions (consumer spending on luxury items) and shipping, which is also affected by economic conditions (increased trade; low energy costs), raises real questions about t rade providi ng much of a boost t o t he eco nomy. Additionally, observers note th at it is u nclear wh ether th e North ern European countries su ch as Germ any are willin g t o tak e step s i n th eir own domestic economies to reduce their levels of savings, curb exports, cut their current account surpluses, an d p romote th is reb alancing wi thin th e Eurozone.[60] Ho w imb alances will be resolve d within th e E urozone m ay be an im portant component of debates about EU integration in the future.

U.S. Economy

In a ddition t o sha ping de bates ove r re gulatory re form, bot h b etween t he United States and the EU as well as within the G-20 more broadly,[61] Greece's debt crisis could have at least fiv e major implications for the United States. First is the exchange rate. Many expect that if invest ors lo se confidence in the future of the Eurozone, and more current account adjustment is re quired for the Eurozone as a whole, the value of the euro will weak en.[62] Already, the euro has de preciated in recent m onths agains t the U.S. dollar (**Figure 2**), falling by more than 15% between Dece mber 12, 2009 an d M ay 7, 20 10, (from 1.51$/€ t o 1 .27$/€). A weaker euro would likely lower U.S. e xports to th e Eu rozone an d in crease U.S. imports from the Eurozone, widening the U.S. trade deficit.[63] On the other hand, it will make purchases and U.S. investments in Eurozone countries cheaper in dollar terms.

Second, the United States ha s a large financial stake in the EU. T he EU as a whole is th e Un ited States's b iggest trad ing partner an d h undreds of billions of dollars flow between the E U an d the United States each year. [64] Widesp read financial in stability in the EU co uld impact trade and growth in the region, which in tu rn cou ld im pact th e U.S. eco nomy. On th e o ther hand, in stability in th e EU may make th e Un ited States m ore attractiv e to inv estors and en courage cap ital flows to the United States. However, if the crisis is contained to Greece, the effects on th e United States wo uld b e sm aller th an in stability t hroughout the EU as a whole.

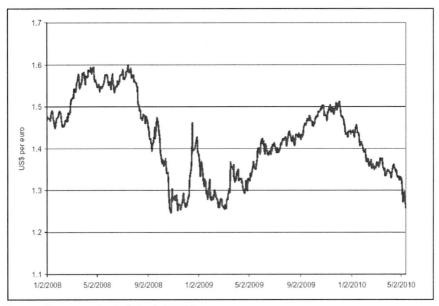

Source: European Central Bank (ECB).

Figure 2. US$/Euro Exchange Rate, January 2008 – May 2010.

Third, a Greek default could have implications for U.S. commercial interests. Although m ost of Greece's debt is held by Europeans, $16.6 billion of Greece 's debt obligations are owed to creditors within the United States.[65] Although not an insignificant amount of money, the relative size of U.S. creditor exposure to Greek bonds however is likely too small to create significant effects on the U.S. economy overall if Greece were to default.

Fourth, the global recession has worsened the government budget position of a large num ber of countries. Some argue that credit m arkets may have awake ned to the magnitude of the debt problem due to the large number of countries that are involved and the extent of the budget deficits. For example, some have argued that there are strong sim ilarities between Greece's financial situation and the financial situation i n the Un ited States.[66] Like Gree ce, it is a rgued, t he United States has been reliant on foreign investors to fund a larg e budget deficit, resulting in rising levels of ex ternal debt and vulnerability to a sudd en rev ersal in in vestor confidence. Others point out that the United States, unlike Greece, has a floating exchange rate an d its cu rrency is an i nternational reserve currency, wh ich alleviates many of the pressures associated with rising debt levels.

Fifth, debates ove r im balances betwee n c urrent account deficit and current account surplus countries wi thin the Euroz one a re sim ilar to the de bates about imbalances between the United States a nd China. These debates reiterate how the economic policies of one c ountry ca n affect other c ountries an d th e need for international eco nomic co operation an d co ordination to ach ieve in ternational financial stability.

APPENDIX A. TIMELINE OF EVENTS SINCE APRIL 22, 2010

- **4/22/10** –Eurostat, the EU's statis tical agency, announces its estim ate of Greek go vernment budget defi cit for 2009: 13.6% of GDP. This is almost a full perce ntage point higher than 12.7% of GDP reported by Greek government in January 2010, and more than double the 6.7% of GDP reported by th e pre vious G reek government b efore O ctober 2009.
- **4/22/10** – M oody's dow ngrades G reek b onds on e n otch a nd places Greece on a negative outlook. Greek bo nd spreads wi den. Yi elds on Greek 1 0-year bon ds rise t o 8. 7%, com pared to Germ any's 10-year bonds at 3.04%.[67]
- **4/23/10** – T he G reek g overnment requ ests to draw o n €45 b illion (about $ 60 billion) in em ergency fina ncial assistance prev iously agreed by Eurozone m embers and t he I MF: €30 billion (ab out $ 40 billion) fro m Eurozone member states and €15 bil lion (abo ut $ 20 billion) from the IMF.
- **4/27/10** – Ratings a gency Standard and Poor's downgrades Greek sovereign debt to "junk" status and downgrades Portuguese sovereign debt by two notches.

- **4/28/10** – Sta ndard an d Poor's dow ngrades Span ish s overeign bo nds one notch.
- **4/28/10** – In meetings w ith M embers of th e G erman Parli ament (*Bundestag*), IMF Mana ging D irector D ominique Strauss-K ahn reportedly rai ses the pr ospect of a t hree-year assistance pa ckage t o Greece totaling €120 billion (about $160 billion).
- **4/28/10** - Fol lowing the downgrade of i ts so vereign bo nds, the Portuguese g overnment re portedly announces it w ill im mediately implement austerity measures initially planned for 2011 in an effort to regain investor confidence.
- **4/29/10** – Greece reporte dly agrees t o t he out line of a €25.6 b illion (about $ 32 b illion) aus terity packa ge, i ncluding a t hree-year wage freeze for public sector workers, in return for a m ultibillion-euro loan from the Eurozone and the IMF.
- **5/01/10** – O ngoing G reek pr otests a gainst government aus terity measures turn violent at times.
- **5/02/10** – The Eurozone and IMF announce a three-year, €110 billion (about $145 billion) stabilization plan for Greece. Eurozone countries are to contribute €80 billion (about $105 billion) in bilateral loans and the IMF is to provide €30 billion (about $40 billion) through a Stand-By A rrangement (SBA), t he IMF's st andard l ending i nstrument. Greece's no minal GDP for 2010 is fore casted t o be €229 b illion (about $ 312 billion).[68] In exchange for financial assis tance, Greec e agrees to aust erity measures worth 1 3% of na tional i ncome over th e next four y ears. Finan cial assistan ce c annot b e dis bursed until parliamentary appro val i s secured in th e ne cessary coun tries (including Germany) and the IMF Executive Board approves the IMF loan.
- **5/03/10** – T he European C entral Bank (ECB) suspends the m inimum credit rati ng require d for G reek bon ds used in E CB li quidity-providing o perations. T his policy c hange aim s to susta in liquidity in the European banking sector.
- **5/05/10** – Three Greek bankers are killed in anti-reform riots.
- **5/06/10** – The Greek parliament pass es a usterity measures necess ary for Eurozone and IMF financial assistance by a vote of 171 to 121.[69]
- **5/06/10** – D ow Jones drop s nearly 1,0 00 po ints in l ess than half a n hour. Initially, observers suspect c ontagion from Greece's debt crisis. Subsequent re ports su ggest that ot her fact ors w ere at pl ay. The D ow Jones recovered to a loss of 347 points at the close.

- **5/07/10** – German, French, and Dutch parliaments approve financial assistance to Greece.
- **5/09/10** – The IMF Executive Board approves the loan to Greece.
- **5/09/10** –EU leaders announce that €500 billion (about $636 billion) will be available for v ulnerable E uropean co untries, with t he IMF ready to provide a n a dditional €220 bi llion (ab out $ 280 b illion) to €250 billion (about $318 billion). This assumes the same division as with the Greek package (2/3 from Eurozone, 1/3 from IMF). The IMF only provides financial assistance to countries that IMF only provides financial assistance, and Greece is the only Eurozone country that has requested assistance to date. The ECB also announced it w ould buy member state bonds, a change from previous policy.
- **5/09/10** – The U.S. Federal Reserve announces it will reopen currency swap lines with other major central banks, including the ECB, to help ease economic pressure.
- **5/10/10** – M arkets react fa vorably to announcement of EU financ ial assistance pa ckage; bond s preads of vu lnerable Eu ropean countries fall and euro begins to strengthen.
- **5/19/10** – G reek de bt w orth €8.5 bil lion (about $1 0.8 bil lion) is scheduled to fall due.

APPENDIX B. ECONOMIC INDICATORS FOR SELECTED EUROZONE COUNTRIES AND THE UNITED STATES

Country	2005	2006	2007	2008	2009	2010	2011
Government budget, % of GDP							
Greece	-5.3	-3.2	-4.0	-7.8	-13.0ᵃ	-9.4	-6.0
Portugal	-6.0	-3.9	-2.7	-2.8	-9.4	-8.5	-7.1
Spain	1.0	2.0 1.9		-4.1	-11.4	-11.5	-9.5
Italy	-4.2	-3.3	-1.5	-2.7	-5.3	-5.3	-5.1
Ireland	1.7	3.0 0.2		-7.2	-12.0	-12.5	-9.8
Germany	-3.3	-1.6	0.2	0.0	-3.1	-5.6	-5.2
France	-3.0	-2.3	-2.7	-3.3	-7.5	-8.4	-7.9
Netherlands	-0.3	0.5	0.2	0.7	-5.3	-6.2	-5.1
United Kingdom	-3.3	-2.6	-2.6	-4.9	-11.4	-12.8	-10.9
United States	-2.6	-1.9	-1.2	-3.1	-9.9	-11.1	-10.8

(Continued)

Country	2005	2006	2007	2008	2009	2010	2011
Public debt, % of GDP							
Greece	114.5	107.9	103.9	102.6	116.3	130.1	136.2
Portugal	63.6	64.7	63.6	66.3	76.9	85.0	91.0
Spain	43.0	39.6	36.2	39.7	55.2	67.4	77.0
Italy	105.8	106.4	103.4	106.1	115.2	119.6	120.3
Ireland	27.2	24.9	24.2	44.0	62.2	76.6	87.6
Germany	68.1	67.6	64.9	66.0	72.0	77.1	80.1
France	66.4	63.6	63.8	67.5	77.5	84.4	89.8
Netherlands	51.8	47.4	45.5	58.2	63.1	67.8	71.2
United Kingdom	42.2	43.2	44.2	52.0	68.1	78.1	84.7
United States	36.9	36.5	36.2	37.5	47.3	54.5	64.5
Current Account, % of GDP							
Greece	-7.5	-11.3	-14.4	-14.6	-11.2	-9.7	-8.1
Portugal	-9.5	-10.0	-9.4	-12.1	-10.1	-9.0	-10.2
Spain	-7.4	-9.0	-10.0	-9.6	-5.1	-5.3	-5.1
Italy	-1.7	-2.6	-2.4	-3.4	-3.4	-2.8	-2.7
Ireland	-3.5	-3.6	-5.3	-5.2	-2.9	0.4	-0.1
Germany	5.1	6.5	7.6	6.7	4.8	5.5	5.6
France	-0.4	-0.5	-1.0	-2.3	-1.5	-1.9	-1.8
Netherlands	7.3	9.3	8.7	4.8	5.2	5.0	5.3
United Kingdom	-2.6	-3.3	-2.7	-1.5	-1.3	-1.7	-1.6
United States	-5.9	-6.0	-5.2	-4.9	-2.9	-3.3	-3.4
GDP, Billion US$[b]							
Greece	243	264	310	352	331	325	321
Portugal	186	195	223	245	228	226	228
Spain	1,132	1,236	1,443	1,602	1,464	1,425	1,433
Italy	1,781	1,865	2,119	2,307	2,118	2,121	2,159
Ireland	202	222	260	268	228	216	222
Germany	2,793	2,920	3,328	3,673	3,353	3,333	3,385
France	2,148	2,270	2,598	2,867	2,676	2,669	2,723
Netherlands	640	678	779	877	795	797	804
United Kingdom	2,283	2,443	2,800	2,684	2,184	2,223	2,297
United States	12,638	13,399	14,078	14,441	14,256	14,800	15,397

Source: Data on government budgets (%of GDP) and public debt (% of GD P) is from Economist Intelligence Unit (EIU) Country Reports, April 20 10. Data on current accounts (% of GDP) and G DP is fro m th e IMF's W orld Econo mic Outlook Database, April 2010.

Notes: EIU dat a for 2010 and 2011 are foreca sts. World Economic Outlook forecasts start in 2008 or 2009 depending on the country and indicator.

a. Eurostat ann ounced at the e nd of April 2010 that their esti mate of Greec e's fiscal deficit for 2009 to be 13.6% of GDP.

b. Net public debt for Portugal, France, the United Kingdom, and the United States.

ACKNOWLEDGMENTS

Amber Wilhelm, Graphics Specialist, prepared Figure 1.

End Notes

[1] Jon H ilsenrath, "Q&A: Carmen Reinhart on G reece, U.S. Debt and Other 'Scary S cenarios'," *Wall Street Journal*, February 5, 2010.

[2] Carmen Reinh art, "The Ec onomic and Fiscal Consequences of Financial Crises," Vo xEU, January 26, 2009.

[3] For more on the global financial crisis, see CRS Report RL34742, *The Global Financial Crisis: Analysis and Policy Implications*, coordinated by Dick K. Nanto.

[4] For the Greek financial assis tance package a nd the broader Eur ozone financial assistance package, the exchange rate at the time the package was announced is used. Otherwise in the report, the exchange rate used is the exchange rate as of May 6, 2010: €1 = $1.2727. Source: Euro pean Central Bank , htt p://www.ecb.int/stats/exchange/eurofxref/html/eurofxref-graph. However, as noted later in the report, currency swings are underway, and dollar conversions of data denominated in euros should be approached as estimates.

[5] Provisional data for end-2009 Q4. Bank for Inte rnational Settlements (BIS), "Consolidated International Claims of BIS Re porting Banks," Table 9B: Consolidat ed Foreign Claims of Reporting Banks - Immediate Borrower Basis, http://www.bis.org/statistics

[6] Steven Erlanger, Katrin Be nnhold, and David E. Sanger, "Debt Aid Package for Europe Took Nudge from Washington," *New York Times*, May 10, 2010.

[7] Ibid.

[8] Kerin Hope, J ames Politi, and Anna Fifield, " G20 to Look at Monetary Fund Initiative, " *Financial Times*, March 9, 2010.

[9] The current account is the d ifference between ex ports and imports , plus net income payments and net unilatera l transfers. By a ccounting id entity, the current ac count is equal to net inflows of foreign capital. Current account deficits are financed by foreign capital inflows.

[10] IMF, *World Economic Outlook*, October 2009 an d European Commission, DG Ec onomic and Financial Affairs, *http://ec.europa.eu/economy*

[11] For example, see "A Very European Crisis," *Economist*, February 4, 2010.

[12] "Country Report: Greece," *Economist Intelligence Unit*, April 2010.

[13] http://ec.europa.eu/economy

[14] For more ab out the effects of the global re cession on g overnment budgets, and how governments hav e tried to addres s these challenge s, see CRS Report R41 1 22, *Limiting Central Government Budget Deficits: International Experiences*, by James K. Jackson.

[15] "Is Greece Heading for Default?," *Oxford Economics*, January 29, 2010.

[16] For example, see Kerin Hope, Quentin Peel, and Tony Barber, "Greece Turns on EU Critics, " *Financial Times*, February 13, 2009 and Louise Story et al., "Wall St. Helped to Mask Debt Fueling Europe's Crisis," *New York Times*, February 14, 2009.

[17] "Fiscal Woes to Do g Greek Bonds Even if Aid Offered," *Reuters*, March 22, 2010. 10 basis points = 0.1 percentage point.

[18] Carrick Mollenkamp and Cass ell Bryan-Low, " Greece Leaps On e Key Hurdle," *Wall Street Journal*, March 5, 2010.

[19] Elena Bec atoros and Melissa Eddy, "Greece Still Under Siege Despite Aid Pledge, " *WTOP*, April 26, 2010.

[20] Economist Intelligence Unit, "Country Report: Greece," April 2010.

[21] At constant prices. IMF, *World Economic Outlook*, October 2009.

[22] *Update of the Hellenic Stability and Growth Programme*, Greek Ministry of Finan ce, January 2010, http://www.mn   ec.gr/export/sites/mnec/en/economics/growth_programme_2005-8/2010_01_15_SGP

[23] Ibid.

[24] A dministration encompasses public services i   ncluding: executive and legislat ive organs; financial and fiscal affairs; extern al affairs; foreign economic aid; general services; basic research; research and   development; public debt transactions and o   ther general serv ices. "OECD Economic Survey: Greece," *OECD*, May 2007.

[25] International Monetary Fund , "Europe an d IM F Agree €110 Billion Financing   Plan With Greece," IMF Survey online, May 2, 2010.

[26] "OECD Economic Survey: Greece," *OECD*, July 2009.

[27] Ec onomist Intelligence Unit, " Country Report: Greece ," Marc h 2010; OECD Economic Survey: Greece , July 2009; and Hellenic Foundat ion for Foreign and European P olicy (ELIAMEP), *Economic Fact Sheet Greece 2009/10*, March 2010.

[28] "Is Greece Headed for Default?," *Oxford Economics*, January 29, 2010.

[29] *Resolution of the European Council on the Stability and Growth Pact*, Amsterdam, June 19, 1997, *Council Regulation (EC) 1466/97*, and *Council Regulation (EC) 1467/97*, http://ec.europa.eu/economy

[30] Europe an Co mmission, *Report from the Commission: Greece*, Brussels, May 19, 20 04, http://ec.europa.eu/economy

[31] European Commission, *Recommendation for a Council Decision Abrogating Decision 2004/91 7/EC 9 on the Existence of an Excessive Deficit in Greece*, Bru ssels, May 16, 2007, http://ec.europa.eu/economy 12_commission_en.pdf.

[32] European Co mmission, DG E conomic and Financial Affairs, *Stability and Growth Pact, Country-specific procedures*, http://ec.europa.eu/economy

[33] On April 22, 2010, the EU's statist ical authority, Eurostat, estimated the Greek gov ernment's 2009 budget deficit as 13.6% of GDP, almost one percentage point higher than the 12.7% of GDP previously estimated by the Papandreou government.

[34] For more detai ls on the Greek government's proposed austerity measures, see Greek Ministry of Finance, *Update of the Hellenic Stability and Growth Programme*, Janu ary 201 0; and *Report to the Implementation of the Hellenic Stability and Growth Programme and Additional Measures*, March 201 0. Both available at http://www.mnec.gr/en/economics/growth_programme_2005-8/.

[35] "Greece Economy: An Austere Future," *Economist Intelligence Unit*, March 9, 2010.

[36] "Greece/EU: Athens Frets under Financial Supervision," *Oxford Analytica*, February 17, 2010. A 2008 reform o f the Greek pension system legally reduced the number of pension funds from 133 to 13 (with five basic funds and eig   ht smaller and supplementary funds). However, some observers hav e noted that the 2008 reforms have yet to be fully implemented.

[37] Europea n Co mmission Economic Forecast for Greece, Spring 2010, M ay 5, 2010 , http://ec.europa.eu/economy "Country Report: Gre ece," *Economist Intelligence Unit*, April 2010.

[38] Hellenic Fou ndation for Foreign and European Policy (ELIAM EP), *Economic Fact Sheet Greece 2009/10*, March 201 0; " Is Greece Heading for Default?," *Oxford Economics*, January 29, 2010.

[39] Hellenic Fou ndation for Foreign and European Policy (ELIAM EP), *Economic Fact Sheet Greece 2009/10*, March 2010.

[40] "Athens Upbeat After Aid Talks with IMF Chief," *ekathimerini .com*, April 26, 2010.

[41] IMF, "Frequently Asked Questions: Greece," May 11, 2010 . http://www.imf.org/external/np/exr/faq/ greecefaqs.htm#q23.

[42] A ndrew Willis , "G reek Loans Will Be R eady in Time, EU Says, " *euobserver.com*, May 4, 2010, http://euobserver.com/19/30007.

[43] The IM F has "preferred creditor status," meani ng that IMF member states give priority to repayment of their obligations to the Fund over other creditors. The United States has n ever lost money on its commitment to the IMF

[44] IMF, "IMF Quotas," March 11, 2010, http://www.imf.org/external/np/exr/facts/quotas

[45] IMF, "IMF Reaches Staff-level Agreement with Greece on €30 B illion Stand-B y Arrangement," p ress release, May 2, 2010 , http://www.imf.org/external/np/sec/pr/2010/pr10176.htm.

[46] "Rebuilding Greece's Finances," *Economist*, February 4, 2010.

[47] "Rebuilding Greece's Finances," *Economist*, February 4, 2010.

[48] Charles W yplosz, " And Now? A Dark Scenario," VoxEU, May 3, 2 010, *http://www.voxeu.org/index.php?q=node/4987*.

[49] Arvind Subramanian, "Greek Deal Lets Banks Off the Hook," *Financial Times*, May 6, 2010.

[50] Ibid.

[51] Sergio Gonc alves and Axel Bugge, " ECB Giv es Greece Verbal Support, Dashe s Rescue Hopes," *ABC News*, May 6, 2010, http://a bcnews.go.com/Business/wireStory?id= 10572470.

[52] Paul Krugman, "A Money Too Far," *New York Times*, May 7, 2010.

[53] Barry Eichen green, "The Euro: Love It or Leave It ?," Vox EU, Novemb er 17, 200 7, http://www.voxeu.org/index.php?q=node/729.

[54] Bob Davis, "IMF's Reach Spreads to Western Europe," *Wall Street Journal*, May 10, 2010.

[55] Saleheen Khana and Kwang Woo (Ken) Park , "Contagion in the Stock Markets: The Asian Financial Crisis Revisited," *Journal of Asian Economics*, vol. 20, no. 5 (S eptember 2009), pp. 56 1-569.

[56] Louise Story, Landon Thomas Jr., and Nels on D. Sch wartz, " Wall St. Helped M ask Debt Fuelling Europe's Crisis," *New York Times*, February 14, 2010.

[57] Nelson D. Schwartz and Sewell Chan, "In Greece's C risis, Fed Studies Wall St. 's A ctivities," *New York Times*, February 25, 2010.

[58] George A. Papendreou, *Remarks on Rising to the Challenge of Change: Greece, Europe, and the United States*, Brookings, March 8, 2010, http://www.brookings.edu/~/media

[59] Philip Whyte, "Why Christine Lagarde is Right About Germa ny," *Centre for European Reform*, March 26, 2010.

[60] Ibid.

[61] The G-20 is a forum for dis cussing economic policies among 20 major adv anced an d emerging-market countries. Follo wing the financia l crisis, financial regulation has been a major topic of focus at the G-20 meetings. For more on the G-20, s ee CRS Report R40977, *The G-20 and International Economic Cooperation: Background and Implications for Congress*, by Rebecca M. Nelson.

[62] Wolfgang Mü nchau, "Why the Euro will Continue to Weaken ," *Financial Times*, March 7 , 2010.

[63] This effect was highlighted by Greece's Prime Minister in remarks at Brookings. See George A. Papandreou, *Rising to the Challenge of Change: Greece, Europe and the United States*, Brookings, March 8, 2010, http://www.brookings.edu/~/media

[64] For more on U.S.-EU ec onomic ties, see CRS Report RL3060 8, *EU-U.S. Economic Ties: Framework, Scope, and Magnitude*, by William H. Cooper.

[65] Provisional data for end-2009 Q4.   Bank for Inte rnational Settle ments (BIS), "Consolidated International Claims of BIS Re porting Banks," Table 9B: Consolidat ed Foreign Claims of Reporting Banks - Immediate Borrower Basis, http://www.bis.org/statistics

[66] For example, see Patrice H ill, "Bernanke Delivers B lunt Warning on U.S. Debt," *Washington Times*, February 25, 2010, and   Anne Applebau m, "America's Debt Spiral Resembles Greece's Crisis," *Washington Post*, February 17, 2010.

[67] Mark Brown , Clare Connagha n, and Katie Martin, "Greek Bon   d Yields Spike to Record Levels," *Wall Street Journal*, April 22, 2010.

[68] Economist Intelligence Unit, "Country Report: Greece," April 2010.

[69] Kerin Hope, "Greece Passes Tough Austerity Measures," *Financial Times*, May 6, 2010.

INDEX

capital markets, viii, 39, 40, 41, 46, 47,
   58, 65, 68, 74, 81, 82
capital mobility, 9
central bank, 2, 5, 7, 9, 18, 23, 32, 48,
   49, 66, 67, 89
certification, 59
China, 26, 54, 66, 87
circulation, 38, 80
civil service, 74, 75
collateral, 18, 47
combined effect, 57
communist countries, 61
comparative advantage, 72, 76
compensation, 12
competition, 6
competitiveness, 12, 13, 21, 22, 39, 46,
   57, 72, 74, 83
compliance, 9, 39
conference, 59
congressional hearings, 68
consent, 50
consolidation, 18, 74, 75, 76
constant prices, 92
constitutionality, 23
consumption, 9, 14, 26, 55, 56, 57, 71
convergence, 7, 12, 34, 73
convergence criteria, 7, 34, 73
coordination, 2, 3, 15, 19, 24, 29, 31, 33,
   87
corruption, 71
cost, 6, 11, 36
costs of production, 13, 85
Council of Europe, 19
Council of Ministers, 31
Council of the European Union, 31, 35,
   73
covering, 52
credit market, 55, 87
credit rating, 41, 66, 69, 70, 83, 88
creditors, 14, 42, 43, 61, 63, 66, 86, 93
crisis management, 16, 29, 34
critics, 9, 79
culture, 6
currency, 2, 3, 4, 5, 6, 8, 9, 10, 13, 14,
   18, 19, 22, 23, 24, 26, 28, 29, 30, 32,

33, 34, 36, 38, 41, 46, 48, 58, 62, 66,
   67, 68, 72, 79, 81, 84, 87, 89, 91
current account, viii, 13, 14, 20, 26, 30,
   35, 52, 65, 68, 72, 74, 85, 87, 90, 91
current account deficit, viii, 13, 26, 35,
   65, 68, 72, 74, 85, 87
current account surplus, 85, 87
current balance, 35
Cyprus, 7, 12, 33, 38
Czech Republic, 33, 38

D

database, 11, 34
debts, 7, 59, 69
deficit, viii, 8, 9, 14, 16, 19, 25, 26, 32,
   38, 40, 41, 43, 61, 65, 68, 69, 71, 73,
   74, 81, 87
deflation, 15
Denmark, 33, 38
Department of Commerce, 34, 56
depreciation, 3, 14, 66
derivatives, 84
devaluation, 10, 14
developed countries, 39, 45, 79
developing countries, 39
digital technologies, 20
direct investment, 6, 27, 52
directors, 17
distress, 29
divergence, 12
domestic demand, 13
draft, 19, 59

E

early retirement, 44
earnings, 27, 75
Eastern Europe, 61, 68
Economic and Monetary Union, 3, 5, 28,
   31, 68
economic competitiveness, 75
economic cooperation, 87
economic downturn, 8, 67, 75